I(V)F
ONLY!

Giving pins + needles a whole
new meaning

Jodie Nicholson

Typeset in Palatino

Editing, design, typesetting and publishing by UK Book Publishing

www.ukbookpublishing.com

ISBN: 978-1-914195-03-7

*To my Husband Steve, for his patience
and unwavering support.*

*To our Family and Friends for investing
in our journey to become Parents.*

*To every Man and Woman out there struggling
with Fertility – This book is for you.*

I(v)F
ONLY!

"An honest, emotional and brutally frank insight into how fertility issues and the process of IVF treatment impact on your daily life, work, relationships, and mental health. This blow by blow personal experience does not hold back! Not for the faint-hearted!"

Linda, Fertility Network UK

"Going through IVF can leave you feeling incredibly isolated and overwhelmed. There is so much to get your head around, and more often than not you find yourself breathless with the fear that it might not work, but having Jodie's book with you feels like having a best friend to turn to. Her first-hand experience of IVF makes you feel like you aren't alone. She explains the IVF process and her journey in beautifully simple ways- just how you want such a complex journey to be explained. Her book is the friend I wish I'd had when I was going through my own IVF journey."

Sara Marshall-Page, Co-Founder IVFBabble

"As Jodie perfectly explains in this book, Infertility is isolating. The frank and honest way this book tackles infertility provides anyone TTC with an all-important friend in a lonely place. I circled so many paragraphs which made my heart both ache in solidarity with Jodie's experiences and feel like it could burst at someone else genuinely being able to say: "I know how you feel".

In a time where fertility still isn't understood by our society, Jodie is shouting her extraordinary story proudly to the world. This book provides a voice to all those couples who feel unseen. Thank you!"

Ellie Saunders- Mum, teacher and fellow member of TTC Community

"This book is fantastic, an open and honest warts and all account of the emotional rollercoaster of an IVF journey. A must read for any people embarking on IVF treatment.

Jodie explains all the trials and tribulations that a woman encounters and the effect it has on a relationship plus the continual strain on trying to maintain a normal life whilst going through a demanding physically and emotional path, not knowing whether if it will be successful as they are no cast iron guarantee's in fertility.

It is such a pleasure for us at CARE Sheffield to hear that we have been able to help a couple like Jodie and Steve achieve their dream."

Joanne Roebuck, Clinic Director, CARE Sheffield.

"Incredibly moving and thought provoking. IVF is often the hardest journey for many partners to embark on and work through together. Jodie's story is one that will resonate with so many families, shining a light on this most intimate of topics. The way Jodie approaches this subject in an open and positive way is truly refreshing, and will give comfort to so many that they are not alone. I know that this book will raise awareness of these vital issues and help those who are currently struggling know that they are not alone."

Alexander Stafford MP. Member of Parliament

I(∨)F
ONLY!

03/01/2019

The Idea

The thought of writing a book had crossed my mind before, mostly for selfish reasons: money, fame etc. and truth be told the blatant laziness the recent festive season had instilled in me meant that the idea of such a mammoth task made me feel slightly sick, or maybe that was the sticky toffee pudding I had just inhaled... I blame Auntie Vanessa.

You see, Christmas Day night, it is a 40+ year tradition of my mum's to visit her best friend, Auntie Vanessa, not her sister as the title may mislead, for a second Christmas dinner. A tradition that Steve and I gate-crash every other year. Part of this tradition includes feasting on whatever leftover delights the Kellys offer up and on this occasion it was Auntie Vanessa's home-made sticky toffee pudding. Now I dread to think of the mess Auntie Vanessa left for poor Uncle Tim in the making of such an incredible dessert, but the result was delightful. So much so that I had craved it every day since, resulting in my beloved Steve driving to the shop at 8pm on a Thursday evening for sticky toffee pudding and custard that I could already guarantee would not be what I wanted it to be.

Due to my recent surgery I still couldn't drive and so hadn't been out for some time; needless to say I jumped at the chance to accompany Steve to the shop – and well there you have it:

Sat in a car-park at 8:10pm on Thursday 3rd January 2019, this book was born

And the recent journal and fancy pens I had been gifted had already insisted their inclusion in my mind.

Steve agreeing this was a good idea solidified the intention. Steve's excitement is fanciful, to say the least, so any kind of positive encouragement meant he truly believed in the idea.

So you could say it was Auntie Vanessa's sticky toffee pudding on Christmas Day, or my wonderful Steve for driving me to the shop for a replica pudding, or the shop in which he had brought me to and the car-park in which I was now sat in, any number of these things could claim a stake in the epi-fanny (epiphany – private joke) behind the book, but I must say, with a heavy sigh that it is none of those things, it was something much more desperate – it was my inability to reproduce and my need to feel like it was for a greater reason, a purpose, as I simply couldn't accept that it just was.

The recent surgery I previously mentioned was what's known as a laparoscopy combined with a hysteroscopy and a repeat HSG, the purpose being to unblock my fallopian tubes.

The tests and investigations over the years had been difficult. 'Scary' probably best describes my main emotion although one word seems an inferior description of something so complex.

Although you can never know for sure prior to any tests, we had an inclination that any fertility issues Steve and I were diagnosed with was likely to be a contribution of mine. Steve already had a daughter and although this doesn't necessarily guarantee he'll be able to conceive again, it gave us a good indication that he was likely fertile.

Eventually, following a Hysterosalpingography or HSG Test (also known as the dye test) it was confirmed that I had two collapsed fallopian tubes, polycystic ovaries and I wasn't ovulating.

Evidently, not one to do things by halves, my reproductive system therefore useless, I was unable to conceive naturally.

Unfortunately, the recent op to try unblocking my tubes was unsuccessful and my only chance of giving birth was now hanging on the hope of IVF.

God I hate those three letters I V F

I Venture Forward – BOLLOCKS!!!

But how? How could I possibly be optimistic at the realisation that my hopes of being a mother were now so very clinical? Uncertain. Hanging by a thread, on the needle of science (pun intended).

"You need to be positive, strong and resilient to tackle IVF."

Yes you do, but first you need to wallow for a while and ask the universe why? And cry and scream and hate yourself and hate the body that has failed you.

I need to do all of this, for some time before I can even contemplate forgiving myself for failing in my duty as a woman.

The unfairness that I had been cursed with a body that had a redundant reproductive system was fist clenching enough without our local CCG giving us a big slap in the face and another obstacle to overcome.

You see, our local CCG stated that anyone living within its locality would receive three funded attempts of IVF. Three chances of becoming a parent, what an exciting prospect in such a hope-deprived situation – a prospect unavailable to us due to the fact that Steve was already a father.

Father to a beautiful little girl that I did not have the honour of calling my own.

Our CCG seemed to think that being a stepmother two days a week equated to being a full-time mother and replaced the whole pregnancy and birthing experience with a desperation for money and a need to defy the injustice.

Appealing this decision was a delay that Steve and I were too impatient to endure. After a four-year battle to conceive and then a two-year palaver of testing and unanswered failings, we finally had the answers we'd been longing for and we were not prepared to allow our CCG to penalise us anymore than their financial ramifications already had.

But how, where, when, were we going to find the money?

My family were as furious as we were regarding our lack of funding. Everyone we spoke to agreed the process was unfair and joined us in our anger. Unfortunately, we didn't need agreement, we needed money.

Steve was supportive throughout but that didn't stop me resenting him at times. I couldn't help but feel like he never truly understood my pain. Although he too was desperately hoping to become a parent with me, he already had his baby, he'd already experienced being a parent. I therefore felt angry and confused at Steve, as if his pain didn't offer the same emptiness that mine did. Could I really begrudge Steve this happiness?

With this mixture of emotions, a cocktail of unpleasantness, came an incredible amount of guilt. Steve was my husband – was I really capable of such poisonous envy? Could I really resent Steve for already being a parent?

I wasn't totally convinced that what I felt was begrudging but whatever it was it wasn't positive. I didn't want him to hurt like me – I wouldn't wish this on my worst enemy – but I just couldn't accept that he fully understood me.

And so continues the bitter taste of the emotional cocktails, a taste that I'm guessing I need to get used to; I know this won't be the last.

I hated how much this process had already changed me.

I hated how unfair my feelings towards Steve were.

I hated how guilty I felt for feeling the way I did.

I hated all of this nearly as much as I hated the financial burden. The decline of funding was weighing down on us.

I needed a reason to blame, other than myself.

If I could help others and make myself feel better it would make this whole situation a little easier to accept.

I absolutely wanted to help others, but I absolutely also wanted it for selfish reasons.

I am a huge believer in fate and I so desperately needed fate to answer for this. Continuously searching for the "why?" and somehow hoping that this book was going to be "it".

So I invite you to join me, on what I imagine will be the hardest journey of my life.

I promise to be honest, to share with you the good, the bad and the ugly truth of IVF and everything it entails.

And for now, my book is my baby!

04/01/2019

Today's Mood – ANGRY!!!

At everything – life, Steve, people that can get pregnant, people that are pregnant, of which there were many, I can't believe how many pregnancy announcements seem to slap me in the face lately. Everyone is pregnant!

I'm angry at everything and everyone, nobody in particular, just people. I'm angry at people I don't even know. I'm angry at myself for allowing this to turn me into something that I'm not. I don't mean angry – I'm angry anyway, just ask Steve; in fact – don't!

I mean this curse has made me unreasonable, judgemental, sad and vulnerable. I am all of these things and I don't want to be.

Infertility is a thief!

Not just a thief of your physical ability but a thief of who you are. It completely consumes you, you feel yourself slipping away. You become someone other than yourself for short periods of time and you continuously battle between these two versions of yourself. Only returning to your original self, long enough to acknowledge this is now your "normal".

I'm angry at the impatience this process has built into my character. The fact I have to now wait until February to meet with our Consultant; I shouldn't have to wait.

Like I'm some higher being.

I'm angry at Steve for dealing with everything so well, at the same time feeling guilty for begrudging him such a blessing. I mean, I most certainly wouldn't want him to feel as much of a failure as I do. I fear that either he isn't coping and simply hides it from me or that he copes so well that he judges the way I handle it. Only for a moment though, as I return to the original me and try to get a grip on reality once more.

Infertility is a form of grief: you grieve for your body's ability (or lack of) yes, but it is like grief in the sense that you never forget, you find short spells of relief throughout the day when infertility isn't necessarily the only thing on your mind, for a moment or so you are free from the burden and feel yourself focusing on something else; not for long though as much like grief, you find yourself hit/winded with the realisation of this inescapable sadness.

I feel myself picking fights with Steve, I can't fight with myself but I know I deserve to be punished for my failings – problem is – Steve gets caught in the crossfire between myself and… myself. I think if I'm honest, I'm also slightly jealous of how well he handles himself. I mean, how ridiculous… really!!!

My sores from surgery are still very much as described. A physical reminder of my recent diagnosis and grief. I keep thinking, questioning, is there really nothing that can be done? I mean surely with modern medicine, why can't they just take out my tubes altogether and replace them? Like a hip replacement. I really am just torturing myself. I don't want to accept my body's failings, I am a woman and it is my right to have children.

I'm angry at everyone who takes for granted the miracle of having a child, forgetting that until roughly four years ago, I was one of those people.

I find myself becoming extremely annoyed at anyone who jokes about pregnancy, although I'm not sure why. People joke about many things, which effect someone, somewhere, yet I take severe offence at this now.

Infertility has turned me into a victim and I hate that!

21/06/2019

The Dark Place

When the idea of this journal came to me, I wanted to ensure it was as real as my experience. I wanted to be honest about how dark our minds can be. I haven't spent much time on it over the past few months and honestly, I just didn't have the strength to relive my experiences every day by writing them down. Some days it was questionable whether I was even going to get through the day and many days, I nearly didn't. But it wouldn't be real if I chose all the good bits and only wrote about those, so here it goes...

The anger still consumes me daily, although it is mainly judgemental anger often tinged with a resentment for injustice.

Work appeared supportive in the beginning, offering me counselling free of charge. I even attempted to return to work back in March. What a mistake that was.

Since my failed return – there's that word again – FAILED – work have been somewhat impatient. I feel the noose around my neck becoming tighter and tighter each time they contact me.

The unfairness I feel towards people for the way they make me feel through ignorance of my situation, is indescribable; I have come to a stage of complete disregard for what people think of me, and I refuse to allow others to continue to affect my mood.

There's no way I can tackle work and colleagues with this attitude.

The anger towards others will never dissipate but the daily stress of work I once thrived on would only act as an obstacle for the upcoming process. My job now is to avoid obstacles at all costs.

I can't afford to simply give up work, especially not considering the cost of the upcoming IVF, and truth be told I love my job, but for now I have decided, with professional guidance, to free myself of the pressure the thought of work burdens me with.

Although it may appear that the dark place I refer to could mean work and although at times the thought of any additional pressure makes me shudder with resentment, it is actually my own mind that has caused me most of the unpleasantness I have experienced.

It has shocked me, the blatant disregard I have towards my own well-being and life, especially considering the offence it causes me to hear of how people take for granted the miracle of procreating and new life.

There have been many days that I have wasted, hating myself and the person I am, the way I feel and think, eating away at me like a cancer. I feel like I have tinted glasses on, and not those of the rose kind. But of a dark, toxic kind, that make everything I see appear miserable. I still have things I look forward to, small things like fresh bedding, new purchases, but it is the thought of these things rather than the actual thing itself, as often much like everything else at the moment, the reality of things I hope will offer a positive lift, actually results in disappointment.

I desperately want the dark filter of my life to evaporate with the rain, but I just can't seem to escape it. It's like it has now become a part of me, like a tattoo I regret but I'm stuck with it.

My February appointment didn't need my toxic glasses to reveal its disappointment. We spent five minutes with the Consultant only to be told he was closing our file and we were now on our own. Why make us wait until now for such non-productive news? Tell me then, in December and allow me these two months to source a private clinic. Unfortunately time was not a luxury Steve and I had, and our Consultant had wasted such preciousness for no reason at all. I needed more, I couldn't accept that the day I had been counting down to for so long was simply a waste.

Steve suggested that we go to the private fertility clinic, physically show up and register with them. I wiped my face and set my mind to the new mission.

Upon arrival at the clinic, I was filled with a feeling I had never experienced before, a new cocktail of emotions, an unpleasant, sour cocktail that I didn't wish to continue to drink. This was it. This was my reality from now on. The toxic glasses soon returned as the receptionist explained that we had to register online. Another door slammed in our face. Another reminder that the dark place wasn't letting go of me anytime soon.

I sharply realised that I didn't hate Steve, although anyone who saw how I treated him or heard how I spoke to him would be sure I did. Although initially easy to presume my hate and resentment could be directed at Steve for already being blessed with the one thing I wanted and needed so desperately. Truth was I hated myself.

I was the toxin. I was the tinted glasses. I was the dark place.

The only way to escape the dark place was to escape myself, I needed to be free of the burden I had become.

Even my attempt at escape was pathetic, twelve tablets in and I panicked; truth is, I didn't want to die, but the sadness and anger had just become so overwhelming that I couldn't rationally process it. Steve was amazing as always and I was thankful I had failed at my attempt. The first time I was accepting of my failing ironically. And let me be clear it was only the failure of suicide that I was thankful for. My other failings still clogged the back of my throat like the sickly, sour cocktail the clinic had introduced me to. A reminder that the hell was still very real.

23/06/2019

Tonic

My saviour was Steve, he was so understanding and non-judgmental. Whether he understood or not, he took the time to listen and try. Admittedly he didn't really understand mental health and it was clear I needed professional help.

My Therapist provided the professional support I needed. She neutralised my toxins and diluted the sour cocktail. She was my tonic. She didn't change my thoughts or emotions, she just made me aware of other approaches. The sickly cocktail was still very much in my glass – my Therapist just allowed me to realise that it was up to me whether I drank it or not. Sometimes I forget, sometimes my dark glasses are on and I'm already halfway down the cocktail before I realise I don't have to finish it. Sometimes I've necked it before I can even process what I'm doing. But sometimes I remember in time. And for a moment I find the strength to look past the dark filter the glasses portray, and I see sunshine outside.

The sunshine shows itself in many ways. Sometimes subtle enough to miss and sometimes so very clear that I have no choice but to take note.

The sunshine seems a little brighter recently.

With the help of our amazing families and some very special friends, we managed to get the funds together to pay for IVF.

We actually sold our home last year, when we were initially advised of the funding situation – although it hadn't been confirmed at that stage that we needed IVF, we had a fair idea and we didn't want to wait for confirmation to start preparing. We were lucky enough to be in a position that afforded us the chance to downsize and release some capital; however, the money we raised, after moving costs etc. was nowhere near enough.

We cannot thank our family and friends enough for their kindness and generosity. The burden of financial hindrance had been lifted.

I still fear for when we run out of money – what happens if we are not successful before the money runs out? A bitter, sweet cocktail that doesn't quite linger sweet long enough for me to fully enjoy it before it pinches at the side of my cheek with sourness. Stinging my tongue with its sharpness.

I'm still facing IVF, I'm still childless and I'm still pissed at the system. But at the moment I find myself slowly accepting that this is my path – and it's OK.

Many months ago, just after my surgery, Steve offered some words of wisdom that have truly touched my heart. At the time I understood what he was saying, but it was just another righteous saying that I had no real interest in; whereas now, the words linger in my mind like a calming sense of peace…

"Stop thinking that you've had the right to be a mum taken away from you – you haven't; we are just going to do it differently."

It doesn't happen often but this was pure genius!!!

Our recent appointment, now with the private clinic, had also offered some much-needed hope.

We were almost there. Not parents – hell no. We still had a mammoth task ahead, but for four years just having a plan seemed impossible.

Our Doctor had offered the answers we desperately needed; most important of them all – a start date.

FINALLY!!!

There was only a phone-call and two more appointments between us and IVF. We had a plan.

Our next appointment would be our last "easy" appointment. Lots of paperwork and formalities, and a chance for Steve to learn how to perform the daily injections. We had decided that Steve would be doing the injections. Not just because I couldn't bear the thought but also because there wasn't much else for him to do, so we thought it would be a way for Steve to feel involved. I know, I'm crazy, but I honestly don't think I could do it to myself.

People often say "you will do it" or "you have no choice" or my absolute favourite "it's a means to an end" – absolute bollocks, all of it. Yes I want to be a mum more than anything in the world and yes I know IVF is the only way to make that happen and yes injections are a part of the process, but that doesn't mean I'm not allowed to be scared. Anything that can make this hell of a process less scary without jeopardising my chances, of course I'm going to choose that.

So my darling Steve needed to learn how to do the injections. Needless to say, he couldn't bloody wait.

The second appointment would be once the drugs had been delivered. I needed to go to the clinic so that they could induce a bleed. The injections had to start on day 2 of a cycle and currently being on day 110, it didn't look like my body was going to cooperate, I mean, why break the habit of a lifetime, right?

We were so close!

The sudden realisation that it was actually happening was yet another cocktail of emotions I hadn't experienced before. Not quite as sour as I had become used to. I was so very excited; after all, the past four years had been a desperate struggle for answers and we now had them. I also felt hope, something I hadn't felt for so long. But I couldn't dilute the underlying taste of fear. I'd spent so long focusing on just getting to this point that I'd forgot what that actually meant.

Just getting here was not enough. I now had to actually go through the physical battle.

SHIT!!!

01/07/2019

Pins and Needles

How the bloody hell am I going to cope with a needle every single day? I need positive encouragement just to go for a blood test. Realistically I know I have no choice and I know I'll do it regardless of the pain, but… what if it hurts? I'm such a wimp. I've waited four years for this and now it's here all I can seem to focus on is the bloody injections (no no not bloody, I hope… oh god, what if they're bloody)?!

I decided, in a moment of absolute wisdom NAWWWWT to read some support groups, hoping that they'd all tell me the injections were a doddle, yeah right… Every single one of the comments I read detailed how painful the injections were. Many offered tips on how to make them more manageable – the fact that people who had experienced the injections felt that others may need "tips" to cope with them did not make me feel any better about the situation.

Some of the tips made me feel even worse:

- Ice the area first – but not for too long as this will harden the skin making it tougher to pierce with the needle.
  HELL NO!!!

  When offering what you think is helpful advice regarding injections to someone absolutely petrified of needles, DO NOT use the word "pierce" EVER.

- If injecting in the thigh, make sure to tense your muscle, not doing so can allow for fluid to gather under the skin and this will burn.

  Sounds great! Sign me up for some thigh burns.

- Bruising and swelling around the injected sight is likely.

  Fabulous! Just what these thunder thighs need – more swelling.

You would think I'd be immune to unhelpful advice by now. I mean, the past six months has really opened my eyes up to how bloody stupid some people can be, not to mention, insensitive.

Some of my favourite comments include:

- Aww you'll get there.

  Oh really? Do you have a crystal ball? Know something I don't?

- I know how you feel.

  Oh ok. Can you not have kids either?

- You'll be fine.

  Wow. You know me better than I know myself.

I just become so numb to these comments and so offended by their ignorance that I created a generic response:

SMILE AND NOD

SMILE AND NOD

SMILE AND NOD

Turns out the actual needle wasn't even the worst part of the injections – nope – the side effects were apparently all the more delightful: headaches, nausea, fatigue, swelling, bloating, mood swings, hot flushes, to name a few. Ironically it appears

I'm going to look and feel pregnant all whilst undergoing fertility treatment to get me pregnant.

04/07/2019

Mother Nature

You've got a lot to answer for, lady!!!

One of the most frustrating things about all of this process is how often the goalposts move. You get a plan together and you feel settled and back in control and then it all gets shuffled around again. And this time I have Mother Nature to thank. You'd think, being a woman, she would understand the torment. It would appear she thrives on it.

The upcoming appointments and start date were now all up in the air.

ARRRGGGGHHHHH!!!

You see, the injections must start on day 2 (the day after my period starts) but with a current cycle of 130+ days we could be waiting forever. There was a tablet I could take that would force a period, meaning (to a certain extent) we could control my cycle and therefore create the start date.

But OH NO! That would be far too easy, Mother Nature had other plans. She had decided to allow us to put plans in place and then gave me my period. The week before I was due to start.

Even two weeks before would have worked (120+ days) but the problem with a period this close to my start date was that keeping the start date as it was wouldn't give this cycle long enough and when we started injections on day 2, my body would still be hormonally in the previous cycle.

The tablet used to bring on the period is taken for a week, so if I start that tablet next week it would mean this cycle will only have been two weeks (this week and then the week of taking the tablet). This isn't long enough to be deemed as a viable cycle.

Mother Nature knows all of this!

So I assume everything will now be delayed, my appointment next week will stay as it is and the drugs will be delivered and we will meet with the nurse and go ahead with the injection tutorial, but rather than starting the tablets immediately, I will have to wait a certain amount of days.

Waiting – A feeling we know all too well.

I feel like Mother Nature has called my body into a meeting and together they have discussed my progress. They've noticed that my emotional state has improved and together they've conjured up a plan to sabotage that.

So I'm currently awaiting a call back from the clinic to advise of the best course of action. And for now, the anger has returned, the cocktail of emotions is one of which I am very familiar with: frustration, anger, unfairness, disappointment.

So let's all raise a glass to Mother Nature! You sick, twisted bitch!

The taste of that all too familiar cocktail lingering all afternoon and now into the evening, thanks to the phone call I have received this afternoon.

We can keep next week's appointment, but I can't start the tablet until day 35. DAY 35!!! Like time is a luxury I can afford.

So our IVF journey has now been delayed by four weeks, not to mention the fact that this now meant I'd be mid-injection phase by September, a busy time for me at work.

My body officially sucks!

07/07/2019

STABBY!!!

"Stabby" is such an appropriate word for how I feel. I'm sick of everyone thinking and often saying "I know how you feel".

Oh do you really?

The four-week delay we were now facing had me in somewhat of a "funk" and I knew I'd slowly escape the miserable grip of my own mind, when I was ready, but for now I was quite comfortable with this pissed off state of misery.

Admittedly four weeks wasn't that long but after nearly five years of desperately seeking Motherhood, four weeks felt like another door being slammed in my face.

Imagine waking up on Christmas morning, excited for a day with your family, treats, gifts, dinner, only to find that an unknown force (or in this case, my pathetic excuse of a body) had decided today would not be the day you were expecting and Christmas would now be delayed for four weeks, with no explanation whatsoever. And then, as if the gut wrenching disappointment wasn't sickening enough, you had to listen to everyone else, who, may I add, are still enjoying their Christmas, tell you how "four weeks isn't long" or "it'll be worth the wait".

JUST PISS OFF!!!

People assume that their profound, often useless, words of wisdom suddenly make all your anger and disappointment and fear go away.

Unfortunately – people of the world – it just doesn't work that way.

People telling me how to feel or what to think just makes me want to stab them. Hard. Multiple times.

I guess they don't know what to say most of the time; it's like when someone you know suffers a loss and you ask if they're ok… DUHHH!

Truth is, I'm not quite sure what I want them to say, I guess I've become so used to hating the world that being angry at everything and everyone is now built into my character.

I feel so judged, not as a failed woman, which would be the obvious, but at the fact I'm struggling so much with myself.

I feel that people expect me to just get on with it, and this offends me.

Maybe it's me that's being ignorant? Maybe I am judging everyone else when actually people are just being genuine.

I want to be positive and relish in the occasional sprinkle of excitement, but I want to be in control of what I feel and when I feel it. I don't want to be told how I should feel or think. If I choose to be annoyed tomorrow, then I want to be allowed to express that. Am I being too demanding? Wanting people to accept my ever-changing mood.

Another thing I have noticed, I over-analyse everything. Maybe I have become so used to the desperation of seeking answers that I naturally apply this feeling to every aspect of my life now.

I can't help but blame my infertility for everything. When ultimately that meant I was blaming myself. I was infertile.

The anger I directed at everyone else was actually the anger and resentment I had towards myself.

09/07/2019

Work

I imagine, for many of us, work is stressful enough without an IVF battle.

I have been in my current role for about eighteen months and I have always been honest about my fertility struggles – you may think that's crazy, telling your employer that you intend to get pregnant but with all the appointments over the past two years and hospital letters that work have requested as proof of absence, I haven't really had a choice but to tell them; after all – the majority of my letters clearly state "Infertility Clinic".

Work were initially supportive, my appointments were covered under "hospital treatment" as per our "absence policy" but following my failed op back in December and the subsequent five month absence, things soon become a little more complicated.

I'm currently back at work but with the upcoming start date of IVF, I'm almost certain there'll be further absences, even if only for procedures and recovery, without considering the possibility of negative physical symptoms.

My absence has already triggered the "absence management procedure" so god only knows what they'll do to me if/when I need more time off for IVF, like I need that hanging over me.

Steve has been his usual, amazing self and we've decided that as much as the wage is useful, particularly when self-funding, it isn't our main priority – it can't possibly be when we are facing what we are. I will continue to be at work, when I can, until I can't and if they dismiss me because of my absence then so be it; we can't afford for the fear of that possibility to change or hinder the way we approach IVF.

Legally infertility isn't protected under The Equalities Act.

With everything I have so far been through, I feel ready for war, a fight for justice and I fear my desire to fight the unfairness may be misdirected. I also fear that the importance of IVF may deflect my armour, meaning I'm not quite as ready for war as what my anger may mislead me to believe.

The more I think about it, the angrier it makes me, the sickly cocktail of anger and unfairness seems to present itself to me yet again, and this is a cocktail I just can't seem to put down. Why can't people understand? This is my life.

I feel like people expect me to carry on as normal regardless of what that does to me mentally and emotionally. It isn't their money that's paying for IVF and it isn't their chance to be a parent on the line.

Work-wise, I refuse to let the pressure of a career have any bearing on our attempt to be parents.

That's easier said than done. Each time I think about it and subsequently stress about it, is a bearing.

I find myself daydreaming about standing up to people. People that dismiss my pain, or undermine my struggle. The empowerment that would give me, and the disappointment when I realise it is only a daydream.

Thursday is fast approaching so my focus remains on that. The clinic appointment that was supposed to be our start date.

A rush of excitement passes by almost too quickly to register, but I'm aware it was there.

12/07/2019

Practice Makes Perfect

Clinic day yesterday, and overall I think it went well. Put it this way, I felt better walking out of the clinic than I did walking in.

Anyone starting their IVF journey, particularly those afraid of needles, I strongly recommend that if you get a chance to practise – take it. Just trust me on this one. I'm not going to lie – they sting like a bitch but I can almost guarantee, your imagination will be worse.

After much drama and fuss (from me, obviously) I agreed to let Steve practise giving me an injection. The syringe was empty but the needle was very much real. We sat for a good twenty minutes – Steve with needle in hand, debating whether this was a good idea. Both the nurse and Steve thought it was – I, on the other hand, felt like a child that had been sent to the Headmaster, that gut-wrenching dread as your heavy feet drag along the corridor, thumping heart and pounding head – all this before the needle was anywhere near me.

I told Steve to "get away from me". As soon as he picked up the needle, he seemed alarmingly close to me and I felt a rush of panic.

I was genuinely in two minds – I knew that if I allowed him to do it and it turned out to be ok, I'd feel a huge relief. I also feared that if it was as bad as I imagined I'd spend the next few weeks in absolute turmoil knowing what was to come and wondering how I'd find the strength to endure it every day.

In a moment of embarrassment (leggings already dropped to my knees) I said "just do it" and turned my head away. As quickly as I'd turned my head I had sheepishly muttered "no, no, don't" and turned back around with my arms in the air as if to high five Steve. Unfortunately, this was not a high five moment and I started to lose patience with myself.

I took a huge breath in and turned away, telling Steve to "just do it"; by this time I think Steve had lost his patience too – either that or he had just realised he needed to be quick before I changed my mind again.

It was in and out like a flash – a flash that stung like a bitch but nevertheless I'd done it! And as expected, my imagination had been worse. Instantly I was thankful for the practice and Steve immediately felt more confident with his duties.

Steve explained that he had become quite anxious during our chat with the nurse; he had expected some form of resistance from my skin and wasn't sure of the correct pressure to apply. It wasn't like Steve to overthink anything so I knew this was my fault. He just wanted to get it right for me, but the ease in which the needles passed through my skin came as quite a surprise to him and he so lovingly explained how it was like "putting a knife through soft butter".

I was just thankful it was done, I obviously wasn't looking forward to the daily injections but I certainly wasn't as scared as I had been. Good job really, as the nurse explained that from day 6 it would increase to two injections a day.

I also had to bear in mind that the syringe was empty and no amount of practice could prepare me for any side effects that may occur. So the fear and dread hadn't completely disappeared, but it was certainly more manageable.

We signed lots of paperwork – after all, our desperation to be parents was also now a sales transaction, a bloody expensive one.

We received a print-out of the schedule and instructions, which I found useful, but we had already decided we were going to make one of our own.

The Temazepam they would be using to sedate me during the egg collection procedure, had to be prescribed so we called at the pharmacy on our way home from the clinic. I'd been instructed to take this (the tablet) back to the clinic with me on the day of egg collection and the Doctor would tell me when to take it prior to the procedure.

One of the key points for me at this stage was to be clear in my mind of the schedule – I seemed to want to keep going over the plan and the nurse pointed out that I only needed to focus on the next stage. If I break the whole process down into smaller steps and focus on what is next, it won't seem as overwhelming – plus, at every stage the nurses at the clinic will remind us of what is next, so I didn't have to feel so responsible for everything, all at once.

Clinic day yesterday and I still have my war wound
– ok a tiny pin prick but nonetheless it was proof of
my battle.

I'M READY TO FIGHT!

20/07/19

Deals on Wheels

The drugs have been ordered (and paid for) and the delivery has been arranged.

My needles, drugs and sharps bins have to be specially delivered by a medical courier as they have to be refrigerated until ready to use.

I felt somewhat relieved when the delivery had been arranged, I was weirdly eager for a speedy delivery, as if this would be an achievement in itself. As odd as it may seem when facing such a huge battle, every tick off the "to-do" list felt like an achievement. A step closer to my ultimate goal.

D(elivery) Day was confirmed for Wednesday 24th July 2019.

I become a little more excited with each day that passes – don't get me wrong, I'm still absolutely shitting myself, but it is satisfying to remember the relief a sense of excitement can bring.

The tinted glasses are off (for now) and this allows me to reflect on some of the pleasurable moments I've experienced over the past few months. It's easy to focus on the misery and despair I've become used to, but it hasn't all been hopeless. We've had some lovely days out and even a few weekends away – all those wonderful memories lost in my mind, consumed by IVF.

Hopefully as the excitement continues to build daily, I can fondly reflect more often. I've been so insistent on telling everyone I'm not ok and seeking approval for not coping that I've lost sight of the fact it's ok to find moments of happiness too. It's exhausting being sad and angry all the time.

Steve also deserves this happiness; he must be exhausted too. He doesn't seem to struggle the way I do but trying to support me the way he does must really take it out of him, especially considering he is such a positive person.

He's currently out with "the boys" and I'm so grateful for that. He needs some time to just be Steve.

Who'd have thought, something as simple as a drug delivery would be the key to unlocking some of the happiness I'd locked away? Particularly considering I'm so scared of the process that follows the delivery.

It must be the feeling of "movement", actually getting somewhere and not feeling so stagnant.

We have our wall planner ready, our drug delivery has been confirmed. Final preparations are now complete!

23/07/19

HAPPY BIRTHDAY!

My birthday was yesterday and I was adamant I wasn't going to let IVF take the shine off my day.

I'm unsure as to whether it was natural hormones or tiredness, but I woke up in a foul mood and spent the day desperately trying to shake it off.

It's as if I know I want to feel happy but subconsciously I mustn't feel like I deserve to be happy and I unintentionally sabotage any chance of enjoying myself.

Steve really tried to ensure I had as fun a day as possible but I just couldn't shake it off. I remember thinking "Is it because of the upcoming IVF?" and in trying to let go of the process, just for one day, I seemed to emphasise its impact on my life.

IVF really does consume all of you. I over-analyse everything and continually question if IVF is to blame.

It's easy for people to say "forget about it" or "put it to the back of your mind for a while" and some days I really do try, but on the other hand I think – why? Why forget it? It is a huge part of our lives now and I'm doing "it" whether I like it or not so why forget it? Surely I need to face it? Rather than using energy to forget something that's happening so soon, surely that energy would be better spent trying to accept it?

I try to do "normal" things but it's always there, in my mind and subsequently reflected in my mood. I'm physically capable of doing "normal" things but emotionally and mentally I struggle to free myself. Maybe I'll learn, maybe it takes practice, much like grief – you never let it go but you learn how to live with it. It seems to have intensified with the upcoming start date.

On the whole, my birthday was a good one. I'd received my gift from Steve last week – he surprised me with dinner at a Michelin restaurant. We are both massive foodies and he'd booked the tasting menu along with the kitchen tasting bench experience. It was amazing. He's so thoughtful. I didn't forget our current situation at all but it was a welcome escape from our reality. We both really enjoyed it and with our wedding anniversary next on the occasion calendar the pressure was now on for me to choose Steve a deserving gift.

Our wedding anniversary was on the 4th August which meant that we could "enjoy" the day before we started IVF and I was looking forward to remembering our love before IVF consumed me.

Although we knew getting pregnant wasn't going to be "easy" for us, when we got married we were still under investigation so those three letters, I V F, although briefly mentioned, hadn't yet imprinted on our lives.

My mum and grandma surprised me with a visit on Sunday. I was so thankful for their company. Steve was still recovering from his night with the boys at lunchtime on Sunday, when the doorbell rang. I would have loved to have seen my face when I was greeted by my surprise visitors, and it would soon appear that my surprises weren't over – whilst upstairs getting dressed they laid out a huge birthday buffet for me, complete with birthday cake and all.

MY FAMILY IS BETTER THAN YOURS!

The day was wonderful – living so far away from them (approx. 60 miles) means I really cherish our time together, particularly at a time when I need my family so much.

Our families have been unbelievably supportive throughout this process. I guess they go through the ups and downs with us.

24/07/19

My Truth

The drugs have been delivered!

I thought I'd be filled with excitement, I was so eager to have them in my possession, like it was another checkbox that I could tick – truth is I didn't feel that way at all.

The van arrived and I felt a rush of emotions, mostly positive. I sat on the sofa watching the delivery driver walk up the driveway, hoping he wouldn't sense my desperation, like it mattered what this stranger thought of me.

He handed me the boxes and left. As soon as the door closed I suddenly felt so alone – I mean physically I was, Steve was at work, but I couldn't fathom that this stranger had delivered such precious items and had no concept of the enormity of the transaction that had taken place between us.

I felt sick!

I opened all the boxes, hands shaking, and laid everything out on the dining table, white boxes full of drugs, clear plastic packs with mixing needles and vials of medication, hundreds of disposable needles… so much I barely had room on my 6-seater dining table. I had hoped that seeing it all would aid processing the overwhelming pressure I now felt.

I called Steve and sent him a photo so he could see what I was looking at. He said all the right things as usual and asked me what each box/item on the picture was. As I talked him through each one, I became so confused and overwhelmed. I needed to call the clinic for some professional reassurance.

The clinic nurse I spoke to was lovely, she explained that rather than trying to process IVF as a whole I should just focus on the task at hand – what was the next step? Just focus on that for now. As she said this to me I remembered a nurse had previously said the same thing. It's so easy to overwhelm yourself by wanting to understand it all.

I realised that I'd been doing this the whole time.

I'd enjoyed writing my book and I had developed a reliance on the catharsis it provided, but I had also become concerned about how "whiny" others would find it, when actually it doesn't matter.

This is my truth and that's ok!

Who manipulated us into following these unwritten rule books of life? This is how I feel and that's ok.

The over-analysing everything had become so overwhelming when actually I just needed to accept that if I feel or think a certain way then it must be correct. Correct for me. There's no answer sheet that some higher power is comparing my truth to.

I need to approach this step-by-step, the way the nurse explained. Emotionally and physically and just deal with the immediate step before trying to process whatever follows.

Steve agreed and we decided to read through the paperwork together and check the items that had been delivered.

So that was my next step, and the only step I needed to focus on. When Steve gets home from work we can check the delivery and read the necessary paperwork.

I boxed everything back up – and put the vials in the fridge (as per the delivery instructions) and tried to focus on tonight's plan, in the hope it would erase the sickening image of the hoard of drugs I had previously sprawled across my dining table.

06/08/19

Aunt Flo

With our start date fast approaching I'm feeling more and more excited as each day passes.

It's only natural for my body to play one last final trick on me before we start and so – the day before I am due to start my tablets, Aunt Flo has paid me a visit - I've come on my period!

In the past four years, I've NEVER had a cycle shorter than fifty days, yet this cycle has only been thirty-four. As shocking (and typical) as this may be, it is a positive thing for a number of reasons; main one being, time. We are now ahead of schedule, we can cut out the week's worth of medication and then the week I'd have to wait for a period after stopping the medication; we are now approximately two weeks ahead. It also means that our IVF will be on the back of a "normal" cycle rather than a cycle that's been medically induced and manipulated. Medically, I'm not sure if this even matters, if it did then I guess they wouldn't use the tablets in the first place, but it gives me another positive to focus on and I'll take what I can right now.

It does, however, mean that injections start tomorrow.

SHIT!!!

Steve and I had tried to remain as calm as possible in the lead up to our start date, we knew what was coming and we tried not to fuss.

The vials needed mixing and we had agreed to do this next week (whilst I was supposed to be taking the tablets) so the fact my period has arrived and the vials aren't even mixed makes me really nervous.

I suddenly feel overwhelmingly unprepared.

Steve came home from work and we got straight to it. We carefully read the instructions and did everything they listed.

All was going well until Steve had to take the head (sheath) off the mixing needles (which was substantially larger than the administration needles).

Three stages into the mixing process and he stabs himself!!!

Well that was it – I LOST MY SHIT!!!

I'd felt so confident in him, when I thought he knew what he was doing. Now I just wanted to strangle him.

I didn't want to make him feel bad and to be honest, I didn't want him to "psych" himself out – I needed him to be confident, even if I wasn't, but his laid back attitude was starting to piss me off.

It seemed, to him, not to be such a big deal and this really bothered me, although to be honest, I knew him flapping would have bothered me even more.

We eventually talked it out and I explained the emotional rollercoaster I was already experiencing; we hadn't even started yet.

I think the lack of control frightened me and showed a vulnerability neither of us had experienced before. He assured me he had everything under control, but as he described how he would "put the needle in and then swap hands to plunge in the liquid" I wanted to head-butt him!

SWAP HANDS????

WITH A NEEDLE STICKING OUT OF MY LEG????

Great Idea!

Is he for real?

He could sense my frustration and he quickly lost patience with me. I think the pressure got to him for a second and I was surprised at how shocked he seemed that I'd lost my temper. I realised that this was a vulnerability in Steve, the more of a deal I made of it, the more pressure he felt and I became increasingly aware that we were both incredibly frightened. I also realised how selfish I had been in assuming that Steve was coping. I vented whenever I needed to without any consideration for what this may do to Steve, or how much pressure this may put him under.

I couldn't hide the fact that I was, now, more scared than ever, of the injections. I totally understand that we both felt the pressure but this was MY body that had to endure these needles and I felt more entitled to be upset, as if I had more right to be scared.

I felt an anger towards him for doing this to me, like it was his fault, when actually, the truth of it was that he was doing this FOR me.

At the end of the day I have two choices: either do it myself or let Steve do it; if Steve was doing it then I had to trust him completely. I had to believe in him and trust that he'd be confident in completing his task, otherwise this just wouldn't work.

We talked it out throughout the evening and to be honest, I'm not sure why, it didn't change anything, I was a nervous wreck and whether it was the nerves themselves or the fact that I had just started a period, I was also an emotional wreck.

Everything had been leading up to this. I was totally overwhelmed. All the calm I had been trying to harness had gone.

Disappeared.

I couldn't help myself.

I was a mess.

I masked my vulnerability with a defensive shield of anger and this made me hard work, not that I wasn't before IVF.

I can see a sleepless night ahead.

LET THE BATTLE COMMENCE!

To anyone fighting this battle, I hope my honesty and detail allows you to find calm and reassurance in the knowledge that you are most definitely not alone.

Everything you feel is normal and it is normal to feel everything.

07/08/19

DAY 2

10:30am

So DAY 1 of injections is actually DAY 2 of my cycle, already very confusing.

I called the clinic this morning and left a message requesting a call back. I want to clarify timings – as I started my period half way through yesterday, I'm unsure if yesterday is actually DAY 1 or whether today (the first FULL day of bleeding) will be classed as DAY 1. This will determine whether I start injections today or tomorrow as injections must start on DAY 2.

Something else now weighing on my mind – Steve mentioned last night, his concerns surrounding what people know and timings etc. I've been so open and honest with people that they will have a pretty good idea of when we should find out if I'm pregnant or not. Particularly those closest to us who know every detail. I'm keen to remain open with my family, for selfish reasons above anything else – I need their support – but Steve and I have always been adamant that we won't announce our pregnancy to anyone until the three month mark; however, even if I don't actually say anything, I'm pretty sure my attitude itself will give me away.

Not really sure how we get around this one.

1:30pm

The clinic has just called me back and confirmed yesterday was DAY 1. Meaning injections start tonight.

ARRRGGGHHHHH

The nurse I spoke to was very matter of fact which I'm grateful for, yet also a little surprised by. It's as if I expect this to be a big deal for everyone else too.

We went through the process together and confirmed when my second injections start (apparently this one has to be in the morning, which we didn't know). We also booked my first scan appointment in a week's time. By which I'll be on my fourth day of two injections.

I'm feeling nervous for tonight, but I'm also aware that the anticipation exaggerates the fear.

I have "butterflies in my tummy" and the adrenaline rush is sickening.

Let's also not forget the shitter of a period I've been blessed with. Mother Nature's parting gift as she hands me over to the medical world.

9:30pm

First one done!

WAHOOO!

Steve got home from work around 6:30PM and went about his usual routine; boots off, shower, PJs, although colourful socks and flip-flops was a new look I wasn't all that bothered about seeing again. It made me laugh, for which I was thankful.

We had a plan in place (previously discussed and agreed) in which we'd decided Steve would take himself off with minimal fuss to "prep" and I would get myself prepared, he'd then sit beside me and wait for me to close my eyes – this would be his cue to stab.

My advice is – don't overthink it. You don't need a plan, you'll figure out a way that works for you at the time, it may even change throughout the process – just go with it. Our plan went out of the window on the first day of injections and it was so much more relaxed.

Being the control freak that I am, and this being our first one, I wanted to oversee the preparation. We even had a giggle about it as we were washing our hands. It was nice. A genuine moment where we both just accepted our own vulnerabilities as-well as each other's.

I could sense Steve's nerves and he admitted he'd dreaded this all day, bless him. He so desperately wanted to get it right for me, and for him – for him to save the headache he knew he'd get if he got it wrong.

We went through the prep together, a step at a time. The original plan of hiding everything from me just seemed so pointless. I mean, the needles are on my bloody dining table – what are we hiding?

Steve struggled to draw the liquid from the vial, it wasn't something we'd thought about too much but it turns out, it is pretty fiddly.

I got into position and we were ready to go.

There wasn't as much delaying on my part as what I remember from the practice, I guess I knew we had to do it so best just to get it done. I just wanted it over with.

The needle isn't pleasant, as you'd expect but it's bearable. The liquid entering your muscle burns like hell but again it's bearable. I instantly got a dead-leg and standing felt stiff. The advice on the leaflets was to massage the area, although tender – it does help, even just to offer a distraction.

I immediately broke down, relief more than anything I think and Steve offered a much welcomed high five.

WE'D DONE IT!

Dead-leg for the next few hours was annoying but I'd take it any day compared to what my imagination had prepared me for.

I was so keen for Steve to know he'd done a good job.

Same again tomorrow.

08/08/19

DAY 3

11:30am

I woke up at about 10:45am and I feel well-rested, like I had an amazing sleep, but also absolutely wiped out. We went to bed at about 11:30pm so not particularly late but I feel exhausted. I'm not sure if it's because yesterday was so emotionally draining or whether the medication is already taking its toll? I've been feeling some really odd sensations in my tummy too, like a rumbling you get when you're hungry except I am most definitely not hungry.

It's exciting, and having not felt this level of excitement for so long, it's refreshingly welcome.

2pm

I find myself sort of looking forward to my injection. Couldn't be further from how I felt yesterday.

Obviously I'm not particularly excited at the prospect of being stabbed but I eagerly await the relief that overcomes me once it's done. The feeling of relief is addictive and I've found myself craving it today.

5pm

Started flagging around 2:30pm so decided to watch TV in bed. I definitely didn't sleep restfully but just lying silently and resting my body felt nice. I could have stayed there all night but I didn't want my nap to affect my night sleep, so I'd pre-set my alarm for 4:30pm. I'm up and awake but feel sluggish and I have a headache.

7pm

Second injection done.

Steve's daughter even helped with this one – when I say helped, she wiped the area with an alcohol wipe and held my hand for the stabbing.

She is aware of what is happening, Steve and I had decided to tell her early on. It was important to us that she understood why I may be physically poorly and/or emotional but also why I may need a little more of Dad's attention for a while.

We explained the process of IVF in a child-friendly way and we told her the absolute minimum so as not to frighten her unnecessarily. From there she'd taken a positive interest in our journey. Knowing she'd be with us this evening, Steve and I had discussed including her as much as we could, if she wanted to be involved, and she did.

I couldn't have asked for a better hand holder.

Following the injection I've noticed a strange tasting sensation, it's kind of like you can taste the medication for some time after the injection is administered. It was the same yesterday. It isn't necessarily unpleasant, it's just odd.

I made the mistake of opening the package of the "trigger shot" just to have a look. JESUS CHRIST! It's like a spear. DO NOT let your curiosity get the better of you. I can't un-see that now and I'd rather not have known.

It's also raised some questions surrounding mixing etc. Which I'd rather not have whizzing round my head. I'm trying to focus on what the nurse advised regarding not thinking ahead and taking each step at a time. The anxiety these new questions have caused has made me realise how calm I actually was today. This offers an aspect of self-praise I've never experienced before. I'm thankful for that.

10/08/2019

DAY 4

Overview

So yesterday was a busy day – note to self – you can't manage busy days – they wipe you out.

We'd planned a family day out to Whitby for yesterday; it had been arranged for a while and we'd known since beginning IVF that there may be a chance that Steve and I cancelled last minute, depending on how I felt.

I woke up feeling OK, I'd felt better but I was OK. A touch emotional but I think that was the stress of having to take my kit with us, on the day out. We had a table booked for 6:30pm so Steve and I knew we'd have to leave the meal partway through to "shoot up".

As we were getting ready we realised this may not be as straight forward a trip as we'd hoped. How on earth do you transport a half-full vial (half-full, definitely NOT positive thinking – unlike the usual association with a half-full reference, this occasion has a much more negative reference - the fuller it is, the more left to use) in a car avoiding spills/ leaks? Steve, in a moment of wisdom, came to a fine idea – we took a small teacup from a child's teapot set and wedged the vial in the centre of the teacup with cotton wool. It seemed pretty sturdy. We then placed this in the glove box and I secured it neatly in place with an umbrella and a glasses case. It wasn't going anywhere. Steve's random creativity made me chuckle.

The journey was difficult. Two and a half hours of sitting still in a car allowed me to really listen to my body, and it was up to all sorts. I felt queasy and uncomfortable for the majority of the journey.

When we arrived I called the clinic. I wanted to ask If I was able to take any painkillers. I'd also developed a headache that I didn't want lingering for the rest of the day. The clinic seemed confused when I explained I was on the injections and wanted to take painkillers – this baffled me, even more so when the nurse explained that she couldn't see anything on in my notes. We soon sussed it out and I was mortified, although also amused. It appeared that in my embarrassing attempt to articulate the name of the medication I had been mispronouncing it.

The correct pronunciation is actually:

Meno-pur(e)

Very different to my attempt of:

Men-O-per

Luckily the nurse found it amusing, as did I.

She explained that I could take paracetamol but that I should try and stay away from ibuprofen. If I was desperate then it would be OK but if paracetamol was sufficient then that would be better. She also said it was really important to drink three litres of water a day and take things easy. I was surprised at the emphasis she put on this but it made me pay particular attention.

Throughout the day I became increasingly tired; we didn't walk much to be honest but when faced with a tourist attraction of walking up 99 steps to view the bay from above, I decided to give it a miss. I didn't want Steve to miss out but he was adamant he wasn't leaving me alone at the bottom so I was thankful when Steve's mum declared she wasn't going to attempt it either. We perched ourselves on a small wall at the bottom of the steps and I was so grateful for the rest.

The afternoon passed quickly and it was soon time to head to the hotel to get ready for the night's meal. Steve and I had always said we wouldn't stay the night as we couldn't really commit to anything due to IVF; Steve also had to work Saturday which ruled out staying over anyway. Steve's mum and dad had offered use of their room to wash and change before the meal.

As they left for the meal, Steve and I decided to hang back to do my injection. It made more sense than getting seated at the table only to have to return to the room shortly after; better to just follow shortly behind.

The injection really stung, maybe because it was the first injection in a leg that had recently been injected (our first double-up, as we now call it). It carried a warm, burning sensation for some time after, which distracted me from enjoying my meal. We didn't stay for long following the meal – I was extremely tired and eager to get home.

The day had completely wiped me out.

10/08/2019

DAY 5

12NOON

I woke up at around 10:30am feeling like I'd done a workout at the gym. I can't believe how weary the medication makes you.

I feel weak and tired and my tummy feels like I've done a million sit ups, I also have severe period-like cramps.

In the forefront of my mind I am aware that the second daily injection starts tomorrow and although excited at the speed in which this has come around, I'm also nervous as to what this means for me physically.

5pm

I went back to bed again this afternoon, initially just to snuggle and relax (I've never been a duvet on the sofa kind of person). I must have fallen straight to sleep as the next thing I remember was feeling uncomfortably hot and checking my phone to see it was 4:30pm. Again I feel sluggish. Steve should be home from work soon and I'm looking forward to the company.

Call me attention seeking but I'm a little shocked at how little of a deal this all seems to be to everyone else. I want to shout from the rooftops that I am mid IVF, I'm not really sure why or what I want it to achieve, but I can't help but crave some acknowledgement.

I'm feeling lonely today, maybe it's because I had such a busy, family packed day yesterday and Steve being at work all day today, but I just want to talk to someone – about IVF. I hate that I've become so self-absorbed but I'm also resentful of the fact I can't offload. Not offload anything in particular, the strange thing is, if I was sad and upset I know I could always turn to Steve or my family, but I just want to chat about IVF to someone.

12MIDNIGHT

Tonight's' injection was the worst one yet, shortly followed by a meltdown. I had expected the injections to get easier – logic would suggest as you become more used to them and as Steve becomes used to administering them, they'd get easier. The fact that they are getting even harder, in the sense that they are hurting more and more, upset me. I became so frustrated, disheartened and honestly I just felt sorry for myself.

It's also really stressing me out that from tomorrow this will be a twice daily occurrence, not to mention the fact that the new injection isn't quite as straight forward as the first ones have been.

My injections so far (Menopur) are straight in – yes you have to draw the medication from the vial but once that's done it's stab, plunge, out, over in seconds. The second injection that starts tomorrow (Fyremadel) has to be inserted at a 45degree angle and Steve has to draw back the syringe to check he hasn't hit a blood vessel, if blood appears he has to discard that needle and start again with a new needle; once we've established the correct position he can plunge the medication in. Although these are pre-filled syringes, meaning he doesn't have to mess about drawing from a vial, the fact he has to draw back and check for blood, frightens us both.

The thought of this makes me feel sick. The injections come with instructions but I can't seem to picture the drawback action and questions arise such as the kind of resistance the plunger may or may not provide when Steve is trying to draw it back, all whilst the needle is in my leg.

There are many tutorial videos available online but of course none of them are for Fyremadel.

I'm really trying to focus on how unnecessary the initial overthinking was the first time around; I am also really hoping that this will be the case tomorrow morning and administration is a doddle.

Alarm is set for 6:30am, on a bloody Sunday (pun intended). My evening injection will continue as before and the new injection must be at the same time every morning, meaning we need to choose a time that suits Steve on a usual workday. 7am injection it is. I fully intend to return to bed once it's done, if that's possible with the adrenaline and hopefully relief I'll be feeling by then.

11/08/2019

DAY 6

12:30pm

Morning injection done!

And yes – we were definitely over-thinking.

Steve says the draw back palaver was easy enough and now he's done one he feels fine moving forward.

The after burn is definitely worse with these ones, but I'd strongly advise to do what the instructions say and pinch the skin. As Steve had to fiddle with the needle, we had already agreed that I would pinch the skin and hold it in a pinched position (obviously looking away). To be honest, it gave me something to concentrate on and although there's more to it, it is over with before you know it.

There's more of a mark left with this injection, I guess because of the angle it goes in at, and it's just below the skin so the evidence of your affliction is more visible. It soon calms down though.

Steve and I went back to bed but struggled to drift back off, I managed eventually and Steve woke me up at 11am with breakfast in bed. I enjoyed breakfast but I'm left feeling slightly sick and still extremely tired. My tummy feels the same as it has. It's definitely busy, working hard. And I'm left suffering because of it.

7pm

Another injection down and another day complete.

Steve and I are getting much smoother at the prepping too, even if I do still squirm as he unsheathes the needle. The injections are still burning, and today it felt as if my skin presented firmer resistance than usual, but Steve says it was no different to the previous injections.

I haven't had the best of days emotionally and for the first time since starting treatment it has rocked our relationship. Not to a worrying extent but certainly to an unpleasant one for us both.

I don't feel or look my best at the moment and this makes me believe, unnecessarily, that I need to justify why, at any opportunity. Steve isn't a talker at the best of times and I had always thought that was just his way; it does make me feel like my politeness in talking to people and sharing my journey is somewhat judged by Steve, like he often disapproves of how much I choose to share with others. Let's face it – I'm a bit touchy at the moment and the feeling that I have done something wrong or that Steve may disapprove only tipped me over the edge. I seemed to use this as an excuse to offload some frustration and upset. As always we soon made up and I think it was important, now more than ever. Steve explained that it's our business and I don't need to justify anything to anyone. I had never really thought of it from his point of view before. I'd been so adamant in my right of free speech regardless of whether Steve wanted his business broadcasting to everyone. It's easy to overlook what Steve must be feeling, mainly because he's so quiet and never makes a fuss but today has brought to my attention my desire to understand his point of view a little more.

This being said, he is absolutely supportive of my book idea, although has made clear he will not be accompanying me to any signings when I hit the big time...

Maybe slightly coincidental that tonight's stabbing felt even more stabby than usual.

Alarm already set for tomorrow morning's injection. Steve is back to work so I will most definitely be retreating back to bed once he's jabbed me.

I fell asleep on the sofa again this afternoon; it seems a daily siesta is very much needed at the moment and to be honest this is a certain aspect of the IVF routine I'll be keen to continue, even after my treatment finishes. I honestly can't remember what it feels like not to be swollen and bloated, it almost feels normal to have a fluttering feeling in my tummy.

12/08/2019

DAY 7

5pm

Fresh out of the shower – what a day!

This morning's stabbing left me with what looked (and felt) like a bee sting. I went straight back to bed and must have nodded off pretty much straight away. I woke up at around 12:30pm, not feeling as groggy as usual – maybe it's the afternoon naps that are to blame for my grogginess. I also managed to venture out to the supermarket this afternoon. Driving is somewhat uncomfortable – it's the position of the seatbelt and buckle mostly but it's tolerable. I also managed to change the bed sheets; it took much longer than usual and my back gave up halfway through but I managed. I feel a whole lot better for the fresh air to be honest and I can't wait for my reward later – fresh bedding!!!

I've noticed I am becoming more aware of how annoying people are. They may all mean well but if I hear the words "focus on your end goal" or "it'll all be worth it" one more time I may not be able to hide the eye-roll. I can't even tell you why it annoys me, it just does. It makes me want to shout "EASY FOR YOU TO SAY". I think as it's such a generic response it makes me feel sort of fobbed off, like there's no real thought gone into their response. On the other hand, I'm not really sure what I want people to say instead. I'm unsure whether it's the hormones or the constant state of uncomfortable tiredness but I'm feeling pretty lousy and miserable. Although the fresh air today offered a much needed boost, I'm still faced with yet another stabbing this evening.

Overall I'm quite proud of how I am handling things. Even Steve has said he's been pleasantly surprised, particularly with how well I sit for the injections. Actually doing IVF rather than just talking about doing it has offered a certain sense of regaining control, and as such I either do it or I don't. I'm almost certain this explains why I'm handling it the way I am. As much as I moan and often feel sorry for myself, you do just have to get on with it. I do still crave the sympathy of others though and I fear my "just get on with it" attitude falsely advertises to others that I'm fine.

It's an absolute rollercoaster; physically, emotionally and I am just about holding it together. Mainly because if I want to be a mum, I don't have much choice.

10pm

I'm all jabbed up, Steve's been fed. My head is banging and my leg is still stinging (it's never lasted this long before). I'm going to bed.

13/08/2019

DAY 8

2:30pm

Took me ages to get to sleep last night. I felt so tired and was sure I'd be straight to sleep but as soon as I lay still, I start to feel all sorts, it's like my mind starts to listen to what my body is doing. The period pain-like symptoms are intensifying and today I've actually felt sick for the first time.

I haven't thought about our upcoming appointment as much as I'd expected, although it offers the potential for exciting news of moving forward in this process; with that comes the gut wrenching reality of having to face the trigger shot and that has really been playing on my mind. I'm thankful that Steve has had some practice "drawing back" to check we haven't hit a blood vessel as this is required for the trigger shot too but I cannot un-see that needle – honestly you may as well ask Steve to stab me with a kitchen knife. It's massive.

Please trust me and don't look at the needle, don't research online, don't even allow yourself to see anything remotely concerning the trigger shot until absolutely necessary. My mind has been on overdrive for the past 24 hours, more so than usual, and for the first time since starting the process I have started to allow myself to explore the more positive thoughts swirling round in there. Nursery themes, colour schemes, even as far as to imagine holding our baby and bringing our baby home. These kinds of thoughts have previously been dangerously upsetting and I've tried to ignore them and block them out. I'm now allowing myself to positively look forward which has been refreshingly pleasant.

One good thing to come out of last night's relentless unrest is that I've finally solved the issue about timing and hiding any potential good news from people until the three month mark: Our immediate family will know the truth, of course, but to everyone else we are going to say my transfer has been delayed. We will say that I over-stimulated so the embryos are ready in the freezer until my next natural bleed, after which I can have the transfer. This will keep people's questions at bay long enough until we can announce.

Sorry, everyone!

Our story is believable and actually a real possibility.

Steve and I both feel positive about this plan and we are convinced people will understand when it all comes out.

On a completely unrelated note – Am I the only person that finds when you put a water bottle in the fridge for a substantial period of time, when you come to drink it you can taste fridge? It's gross. It also means I now need a new water bottle. My fridge is clean – don't judge. But I can just taste fridge, there's no other way to describe it. I'm really trying to stick to my three litres of water a day and this is just not helping at all. Nor is it helping the sickness.

So there you have it – of all my IVF advice, one to remember – don't put water bottles in the fridge or else they'll taste like fridge. You can thank me later.

10:30pm

My tummy is huge, and sore. I'm so done with these injections, here's hoping the clinic tell me I'm done during my check up tomorrow. It isn't often likely that you'll be ready by your first check-up but with me already being at risk of hyper-stimulation (due to my already good ovarian reserve) it is possible.

I'm now excited for our appointment; it's another step in the process which can only be a positive. I spoke to my mum this evening, only via text but still, I thank her for my recent change in mood. She's feeding the attention and sympathy I've so desperately craved and her GIF game is strong (private joke)!

I'm also pretty sure that I'm getting better at the daily stabbings; I still want it to be over ASAP but I do feel much better about them and how I am coping with them. I've learnt that this process has such an ever-changing effect on your mood, it's so emotionally draining, and you really do just have to take a day at a time. If you have a shit day, so what? Don't beat yourself up about it. Try to remember for every bad day there'll be a good day too.

I need to bookmark this page for myself, for the next time I feel a meltdown coming.

It's so easy to say, I struggle with it too, especially on a bad day.

Let's hope tomorrow brings news that allows me to continue this positivity.

14/08/2019

DAY 9

5pm

All in all a great day at the clinic; I'm responding well to the drugs, 17 follicles are growing and maturing (8 in one ovary and 9 in the other ovary) which is good news. Although I'm not quite ready. The follicles need to reach a size of 17mm to be deemed mature enough and currently the 17 that are responding range between 8mm – 13mm. There are some follicles that haven't responded which is totally normal; I'm massive as it is – can you imagine if they'd all responded? I'd look like a whale, not to mention the fact it would take them a week to harvest them all. It's also a good sign for any future cycles of IVF, if required, that I still have follicles carrying eggs that may respond next time.

So for now I have to continue with the injections and return to the clinic for a check up on Friday. If all goes well we are expecting egg collection to be on Monday but this will be confirmed on Friday. If that's the case it would mean only two more days of jabs, trigger shot Saturday ready for egg collection, the end is in sight. Although you can see how confusing this all is.

I also feel really good for Steve, I know he doesn't show it and he certainly doesn't talk about it often but he has subtly questioned whether he has been correctly administering these injections and today's news confirmed that he has.

I feel overall positive, it's reassuring to hear that my body is doing what it's supposed to (for a change) and to have an end in sight is such a huge relief. Even a worst case scenario of not being ready on the Friday would mean another check-up Monday and egg collection on Wednesday so either way there's a week left, at most.

I'm so thankful to be off work – I couldn't cope having to juggle work and IVF schedule let alone adding the physical side effects into the mix.

More than anything, I feel so bored lately, I'm tired and uncomfortable which makes me reluctant to make plans but I'm also bored of TV and sleep. The weather isn't great, in fact it's bloody awful so I can't even go for a gentle stroll, and to be honest when faced with having to get dressed and make myself look human I'm not sure if I can be arsed. Times like these I miss living close to my family, I can't just pop round for a catch up and it's a long way to ask them to drive just for a coffee. Think I'll have a bath tonight, a bit of a pamper session, although it never ends up being that; the idea of a bath always seems more appealing and luxurious than the actual event. I envisaged a movie-like setting, bubbles, candles, face mask, the full works and what I end up with is a few suds clinging to the edge of the bath, no candles because I always forget and actually, what's the point? I last 15 minutes and get bored! My excitement for the day will be the same as it has been, every day for the past week – the relief I feel once my stabbing has been completed and I can tick another one off the schedule!

Rock and roll!

10:30pm

Bit of a giggle during tonight's stabbing. When Steve mixed the vial for the first time and accidently stabbed himself, it really frightened me, and every night (and now morning) since then when he preps my injection I say "Be careful, babe". I didn't really notice until this evening just as we were washing our hands together over the sink, he leaned to me and gave me a nudge with his shoulder to get my attention. As I looked at him, he said, with a cheeky smile "Don't worry, babe, I'll be careful". As soon as he'd said it, we both belly laughed, I knew exactly what he was getting at and his sarcastic humour offered a genuine giggle for us to share. It was nice.

Following my stabbing Steve kindly pointed out that my coping strategies are somewhat amusing. You see I'd unintentionally adopted a breathing style to assist me whilst Steve plunged the medication into my leg. A breathing style that, ironically, you typically see on TV programmes/films of women in labour, you know what I'm talking about "panting" … for a chuffing injection. Man alive – I'm a wuss!

Steve took great pleasure in mocking me and to be honest I struggle to see how he manages to keep a straight face at the time. He must be desperate to burst into laughter but always remains calm and collected. Problem is, now I know, it will make for an interesting twist on our usual routine. I certainly can't do the panting without laughing.

15/08/2019

DAY 10

11am

A stress I never considered in all of this was Steve's work. I always knew my work may offer a little pressure somewhere along the path, even if only for juggling appointments. However, I'd never really considered the fact that Steve would also need a lot of time off and would his work accommodate? Thankfully they have but it offered a new potential pressure to us that we didn't handle very well. We shouted and argued and to be honest I think we were looking for an excuse to release some tension and this was it.

This process is so emotionally draining and even those that are capable of controlling their emotions, can feel fragile, not that I've ever been one of those people – Christ, I cry at any slight inconvenience to my usual routine, God forbid something catches me off guard. Once I'm in that headspace I can be so irrational.

I feel the lead up to IVF intensified these emotions but when it actually came to IVF itself, whether it's the hormones or the pressure of responsibility, but I feel I have been less irrational since starting IVF.

Physically I'm still struggling – it hasn't necessarily intensified lately and it hasn't particularly gotten worse, it just hasn't gone away. It's manageable but unpleasant.

Hopefully today could be my last full day of jabs… I mean, yes I'd still have tomorrow morning's stabbing and the trigger spear on Saturday but still – I prefer the sound of my original statement!

The end is near.

10pm

My god I hope tomorrow they tell me I'm ready, there's no way I can do another stabbing after tonight's fiasco.

Ironically another row with Steve has resulted in the worst stabbing yet – should I be concerned? I felt the needle softly touch my skin and for a second I thought I'd gotten away lightly tonight... boy was I wrong. The pressure of the needle intensified and I realised it hadn't yet penetrated, and then pop, I felt it, like a straw piercing a carton of juice, a sharp straw! I let out an almighty scream (along with a few swear words)! Steve removed the needle and for the first time, there was blood. I immediately broke down. Steve tried his best to comfort me and I could tell he was genuinely sorry, he explained that this was the most resistance he'd ever experienced, I know he felt bad but it wasn't his fault.

My entire leg has felt tender since, as if it could be bruised. Visually you'd never know of such an event, but I wouldn't be surprised if I have a whopper of a bruise tomorrow.

I'm so ready for bed, although I'm not sure how I'm going to rest with this dead leg – honestly the pain and tenderness is on another level. I'd take a swollen tummy any day over this.

16/08/2019

DAY 11

10:30am

Egg collection Monday which means injections as normal today and tomorrow and then trigger shot tomorrow night, injection-free day Sunday then egg collection Monday. I've got one currently at 19mm!!! No wonder I'm uncomfortable, there's some fluid in my ovary which will need investigating during Monday's procedure, could be nothing – sometimes when the follicles become so full they can leak, which is fine. There is, however, a chance that transfer could be delayed to allow time for me to undergo surgery to drain the fluid! After which I'd have a frozen transfer, but that is worst case so I'm not even going to worry about it.

After my scan the nurse went through everything with us, she explained that Steve would give a fresh sample on Monday which means no sex over the weekend…

I thought it was a joke!

I was like "Look at me!!!!!!"

You couldn't pay me.

Seriously who is that warning for? What woman is up for a quickie at this stage in the process? Furthermore, what woman is capable? Not to mention what guy is thinking "Mmmmm I just fancy a bit with that bruised up whale?" Needless to say there's no risk of that in the Nicholson house this weekend.

I feel positive.

Ready!

One and half days left of needles, well, needles in my thigh at least.

Monday is a whole different ball game. Think needles in your thigh are bad! Try needles in your nunny.

8pm

I've been experiencing a strange sensation for a couple of days but couldn't quite put my finger on it; only today, as it's intensified slightly can I notice enough to describe it. It's my whole core, between neck and knickers but I'd say above my belly button, as below that, all I feel is bloated. It's like a tightness, as if I have a corset wrapped tightly around my body, and also an indigestion-type feeling on my right side but as if it's behind my chest, not quite in my back. It's odd but not particularly painful.

I finally had that bath I'd been thinking of, it was exactly how I expected it would be... not at all luxurious and to be honest, the fact I have to lift my tummy to wash my body didn't exactly feel glamorous. I feel better for the bath and the face mask, but I wouldn't go as far as to say "pampered".

Craving stodge; cake and chocolate and lots of other naughty goodness. I know I'll be sorry afterwards and I couldn't even tell you exactly what I want. I certainly can't be bothered to cook tea but I do feel like I owe it to Steve to provide a decent meal, especially considering he's worked all day.

Steve cannot cook, bless him, he'll try but unless it's an omelette or beans on toast he's not great. Don't get me wrong, he'll quite happily stick something in the microwave, he doesn't ever complain if I don't cook, but I do feel a bit guilty. Not guilty enough to actually get off my arse but even so… I'm kidding.

As Steve would say, when he's hinting he's hungry – I'll go and wow him in the kitchen. What he actually means is "Don't bite my head off but you still haven't fed me and I'm hungry"!

17/08/2019

DAY 12 - TRIGGER SHOT

1pm

Slight discrepancy around how to administer the trigger shot.

The instructions provided with the medication instruct administration similar to that of my morning injection... 45 degree angle, draw back to check for blood, plunge. However, the notes/ instructions provided by the clinic advise to insert at a 90degree angle and plunge, no drawback. Obviously this is much easier, similar to my evening injection, but which instruction do I follow?

I decided to call the nurse support number. I'm reluctant as the clinic is closed so it will be a nurse on call, at home, that I will be disturbing and all my paperwork says only for emergencies. Everything I've read regarding the precision required for this trigger shot suggest that it's imperative we get this correct – sounds like an emergency to me.

The nurse was lovely, as they always are. She explained it's highly unlikely we'll hit a blood vessel so a 90degree angle without drawback is fine. I've been doing both, or rather Steve has, so it wouldn't have mattered really but this way is much easier.

So only two more stabbings left; 7pm for my last evening jab and then the trigger shot at exactly 10:15pm.

You can't premix the trigger shot either, it has to be "mix and jab" at precisely the advised time. I feel this is extreme pressure and responsibility to put on someone, especially at the end of all the jabs as you don't want to do this incorrectly and it all have been for nothing. At the end of the day we've done nearly two weeks' worth of stabbings, all correct; this is just another one.

I'm also pretty much convinced the fluid is nothing to worry about – I know I said I wasn't even going to think about it but I just can't help myself, and to be honest I'm thankful because the more I have thought about it, the more I've remembered and realised there's not much of a chance that any liquid could have gotten in my tubes. I have had two dye tests previously and both were unsuccessful because they couldn't get the dye into my tubes, even with applied pressure. My surgery in December was unsuccessful as my surgeon couldn't get anything in my tubes, fluid, surgical instruments, nothing, he actually said my tubes were irreparably damaged with scar tissue and he couldn't get anything in them. I'm pretty sure it's going to be fine.

The countdown for 10:20pm is on – when it's all over and the stabbings are complete.

7pm

Final evening injection done!

Only trigger shot left to do and then I'm free, of daily stabbings and bruised thighs.

Roll on 10:20pm.

10pm

Excited, nervous, anxious, three of the main ingredients of tonight's cocktail.

The past hour has dragged like you wouldn't believe. I know we have a few things to do with the prepping and mixing, but we can't prematurely tick these off the "to-do" list. Instead I'm sat impatiently allowing our task to chip away at me like a woodpecker on a tree…

10:30pm

Those last ten minutes really creep up on you and no matter how prepared you think you are, with the pressure of specific timing you'll feel it; even Steve did. You think five minutes to prep and mix is plenty but when the syringe doesn't take up all the liquid and you're looking at the clock and it's 10:13pm, I don't care how chilled out you think you are, you will flap. Steve was amazing as always. I absolutely couldn't have done any of this without him.

We did it!

Don't be afraid of the needle itself, it looks daunting but it's no worse than any of the others; it's no better, but it's certainly no worse.

I feel free – still shaking from the pressure and adrenaline but the high of this relief is like no other.

No more injections!!!

19/08/2019

Egg Collection

Where do I begin?

Yesterday was wonderfully "normal". Apologies for the lack of journal entry (sorry not sorry) but I was busy enjoying life – injection-free life.

We didn't do much, little bit of retail therapy, it was just so refreshing to enjoy a day not consumed or controlled by IVF and scheduled injections. I didn't forget IVF but the break from schedule allowed me to "breathe". My physical symptoms didn't change much following the trigger shot so I still felt uncomfortable, but it was manageable.

The upcoming procedure didn't play on my mind as much as I had expected – there was some form of anxiety lurking at the back of my mind but it seemed quite a well-controlled emotion (which is new to me).

Monday morning soon came and I woke feeling slightly more anxious but eager to get it done. Not necessarily excited, just keen for it to be over.

We set off in plenty of time and arrived early, by about ten/fifteen minutes. My procedure was scheduled for 10:15am, therefore we had been advised to arrive at the clinic for 8:30am.

As time moved forward I became increasingly nervous but all still portrayed in a calm exterior, I was ok.

The fluid situation played on my mind so although scared for potentially disappointing news, I was eager for answers.

We took our sharps bin to the clinic with us. I was excited to say goodbye to that ugly yellow container – not the lovely sunshine colour you usually associate with yellow, this was more of a harsh, gaudy yellow that you couldn't avoid, no matter how much you tried and let's not forget to mention the "evil" contained inside it. The clinic would dispose of this correctly for us and I was extremely happy to hand it over at the first chance we got. It marked the end of a love/hate relationship for me – in that I hated the injections and the panic it instilled in me, even right up to the end, but I loved the sense of relief it gave me when I'd completed each one. Not to mention the achievement and self-pride I felt when we got to Saturday night and I knew I had no more.

I'd completed what I thought to be the hardest physical part of IVF, certainly the part most commonly associated with IVF, and the one I'd dreaded the most… Until this morning.

I couldn't seem to put to rest, the thought of those two local anaesthetic injections in my cervix – I mean, there's nicer ways to spend a Monday morning.

We were taken straight to a recovery room and advised to make ourselves comfortable (easier said than done when you're about to lie spread eagled, naked from the waist down, in a room full of strangers, with a huge spotlight shining on your vajayjay)!!!

The recovery room was very clinical, white walls, basic furniture, dull with the glaze of dread deriving from the very pit of my stomach, small but ample room for its requirements.

I perched on the "comfy" armchair and left Steve on the typical high back chairs you expect to see in a hospital. We were advised that the room was ours for the entirety of our time at the clinic, meaning we could leave everything in there as we'd be returning following the procedure.

We met with the Doctor and had to answer some general medical questions with the nurse. As well as completing usual observations before a procedure – blood pressure, pulse, etc. – I also had a cannula fitted. You'd think I'd be a pro at needles by now, but I still looked away and gave the usual performance.

The clinic provided scrubs for Steve, not his best look… and a lovely fluffy towelling robe for me, much like the ones you'd expect at a spa – if only!!! This wasn't a spa at all.

Steve then went to do his bit, whilst I had to do mine, and boy how different those two things were.

Mine was a suppository, yep, a tablet for your arse, and not exactly a small tablet I may add.

It wasn't that bad to be fair, you do it yourself, in the toilet, obviously, and it's fairly easy (don't judge). Now I promised to be honest, the good, the bad and the ugly so if you're still reading this far into the book, I feel I owe it to you to continue the honesty…

As soon as it was in, I needed to poo. And the next time I went for a wee (I had to empty my bladder before the procedure, and typical of me to do ten nervous wees before the procedure anyway) but the first wee following the suppository, with little intention, or persuasion, I pooed.

I panicked.

Would this effect my suppository? Should I tell the nurse? There's a conversation we'd all like to have…

It was fine, the nurse said, it should have all absorbed anyway so nothing to worry about. I felt so much better for it. Now time for my sedative, and Steve returned shortly after (not too shortly after!!!!).

The sedative made me feel a little drunk, particularly if I stood up or moved about but nowhere near as sedated as I had hoped. I was hoping I'd be so far gone, they'd have to carry me in.

I was ready!!!!! I couldn't have felt less ready!!!!!

When I first walked into the theatre room, it was quite overwhelming – lots of people in the room but I had a support nurse by my side the whole time – she talked me through each stage and supported me emotionally throughout the procedure; she was amazing.

I was given gas and air from the get-go and I'd strongly advise if you have access to it, use it. Not just as a form of pain relief but I was thankful for the distraction, concentrating on my breathing and having something to bite (although I'm not sure that's what it's for) meant I hardly felt those local anaesthetics I'd been so focused on. Don't get me wrong – you're still fully aware that a Doctor is chin deep in your Nunny but I couldn't tell exactly what he was doing. From then on I felt movement and pressure but nothing specific. Some parts of the procedure are more uncomfortable than others as the pressure intensifies but the nurse would remind me to use gas and air and the distraction would help.

My right ovary seemed to want to play silly buggers and the Doctor struggled to extract everything he needed as the ovary moved; my support nurse therefore had to push hard on my tummy to hold the ovary in place. I asked if Steve could stand by my side for this, he'd been patiently sat at the back of the room up until this point.

This particular part of the procedure was hideous. It filled me with memories of the dye test I had years ago – just more intense, the pressure was unlike anything I'd felt before, but it was over pretty quick and I was keen for them to extract as much as possible.

They then performed a scan to check over the fluid – after a few minutes of tense silence they confirmed that it was nothing to worry about and at about the same time the embryologist had news from the lab – they'd extracted 10 EGGS!!!!!!!!!!

OH MY GOODNESS!!!!!!!!!!

10!!!!!!!!!

I could not contain my joy and relief and I shed an un-dignified tear – all whilst still spread-eagled with my nunny out.

The team congratulated us and advised it was a very impressive count – the average is around 5.

I thanked them all – and I genuinely meant it – before being led back to the recovery room.

The Doctor and embryologist checked in with us during recovery and the nurse carried out more observations. We were advised that we actually had 11 eggs but 1 had broken/split – which was normal.

10 eggs!!!

The embryologist confirmed that she would call tomorrow to advise how many had fertilised, she'd then call again Thursday with an update and transfer was expected for Friday (TBC on Thursday).

I wanted to shout from the rooftops – we'd done it!

The crappy physical stuff was now complete and the procedure had been a success. I could not have been happier in that moment and I cried whilst in the recovery room, out of pure joy and relief, a cocktail I hadn't experienced for a very long time but one I wanted to enjoy and savour.

As the drugs wore off, I felt tired, and more aware of the period pain-like feeling. All bearable though and to be honest nothing was going to dampen my spirits.

Expect to bleed a little, nothing concerning though, maybe take a pad with you, was the advice given.

I couldn't wait to share the news with our family but I became increasingly tired as time passed. It was about 3:30pm by the time we got home and I was starving. I had a sandwich, more out of ease and speed of making than anything else.

When we finally sat down after stuffing our faces it was about 4:30pm and I was knackered. I really wanted to stick it out though and thought that if I could just hold on until 7pm I could get an early night and hopefully sleep through.

By 5:30pm I was nodding off on the sofa, which given how uncomfortable I felt anyway, wasn't the most pleasant of positions to drift off in. I just couldn't fight tired anymore. I left Steve downstairs and went to bed.

BIG MISTAKE!

It's now 11:30pm and I'm downstairs with a cup of tea, still buzzing from today's success. I think my body is so used to short sleeps and daytime naps that it must think I've had enough rest for now. I'm OK with it though, I'll watch a bit of TV and hopefully feel sleepy again soon.

Although the buzz of today may offer some pleasant resistance.

WE DID IT!!!

20/08/2019

How do you like your eggs in the morning?

FERTILISED.

I barley slept last night, with excitement for today's news. The clinic called around 9:30am!

We have 6!!!!!!!

This is fabulous (although does leave a touch of disappointment that we lost 4).

Further update on Thursday ready for transfer on Friday.

I called Steve right away. Much like me, he felt slightly downcast that we lost 4 but overall excited.

You can't help but be reminded just how precious and fragile this process is, just like that we'd lost 4, it offers a new sense of dispirit, not severe enough to override the joy and excitement but it's there.

I suddenly feel extremely protective, much like a mother to her child. I want to call the clinic and tell them to look after our embryos and check they are ok. I wonder if they allow visiting times. To a freezer???

Of course they're being looked after, following yesterday's procedure there is absolutely no doubt in my mind that our precious treasure is in the best hands possible.

The effectiveness and fluidity of how that theatre team worked together was truly impressive. Really makes you realise and appreciate the miracle workers they are.

My spirits are high today; physically I am ok, still sore but managing on paracetamol.

Excitement overcomes me in rushes, we are so very close, and so very lucky to have been blessed with such promising numbers.

21/08/2019

Necessary Pessary

Of all the things to struggle with along this journey, I did not expect a pessary to be one of them.

Today I started my progesterone pessaries. For some reason, medical experts have found that an IVF pregnancy (implantation) doesn't trigger the increase in the body's progesterone levels as a "normal" conception would; therefore, as part of the IVF process, I must take a progesterone pessary three times a day from two days post-egg collection until either a negative pregnancy test or a certain point in the pregnancy (decided by the Doctor).

Progesterone helps thicken the lining in the uterus and so is a really important factor during implantation.

I'd been advised that some "leakages" are expected, as my body absorbs what it needs from the tablet and discards the rest, so it was therefore recommended that I wear a pad for the duration of the pessaries and if I notice any discharge (awful word by the way) not to panic, it's totally normal and my body will have absorbed everything it needs.

I gave the pessary barely any thought – three times a day was slightly inconvenient and I can't say I'm a fan of pads but that was about all the thought I had given this, I certainly wasn't worried or concerned about the application.

Well I should have been…

Not worried as such, but what a bloody performance, Christ, you'd think I'd never done one before.

The applicator is a straw-like device (as in a drinking straw) with a little button on the end and you kind of wedge the tablet on the end of the straw, insert the applicator as far as you can then push the button to release the tablet.

Easy peasy!

Not so much…

Four attempts it took…

Every time I removed the applicator, the tablet was still there, LAUGHING AT ME!

I'd wedged it in to the top of the straw a bit too tight; however, if you don't wedge it in enough it wobbles and falls as soon as you move your hand to insert it.

I couldn't even tell you what I did to eventually master this. I have no idea of the correct amount of "wedge" required, even now.

I think this one may take some practice, but at three times a day I'm sure I'll be a pro in no time.

It doesn't hurt at all, you barely feel it, similar to inserting a tampon, but the frustration this tiny vajayjay tablet caused was quite comical.

22/08/2019

Numbers

I'm annoyed with myself for allowing the hate and ignorance of others (strangers in fact) to take away the buzz of this stage.

I'm annoyed with myself for lowering myself to even responding to these people.

Last night I'd seen a post regarding IVF and the funding dilemma, on social media. Through sheer stupidity, I wasted time looking at the comments, as if I wanted to see some form of approval or agreement for the way I feel about it. I would seriously advise against looking on social media regarding anything that may be personally sensitive as it can be extremely hurtful.

I felt anger at the offence these strangers caused me, and to be honest I was shocked by their ignorance. Once I'd felt that anger, I was hooked, I just couldn't let it go, I needed to put these people right.

In the end it only made me feel worse, the hate grew and the ignorance of people continued to shock me.

This morning, although still reeling from the things I had read, I really tried to just let it go; it festered for a while, like a toxicity that poisoned my thoughts, but it didn't last long...

I got the call!!!

We still have 6!!!

The embryologist said all 6 were really strong and developing nicely.

Transfer booked for tomorrow at 2:30pm so I needed to arrive at the clinic for 2pm.

The embryologist explained that she would give us another numbers update when we arrived for the procedure. Apparently, DAY 4 is a big day and it can be quite confusing and upsetting if we receive numbers in the morning saying one thing and then when we arrive at the clinic the numbers may change. I completely understand this and totally agree that the one update on arrival is sufficient. She went on to explain that things can change quickly and only 1 in 4 couples are lucky enough to have embryos left to freeze after treatment. This concerned me as it was as if she was pre-warning me, as if it's likely, but she did also state that she has to make me aware and be realistic although it's also good to be positive, and our embryos look good and strong and are developing well. I guess they have to say that to cover themselves and explain every possibility.

I'm holding onto the fact that the odds have been in our favour since Monday's egg collection and we were above average from then – surely that increases our chances? I hope…

You may wonder, why the numbers are so important to us?

If we are lucky enough to have embryos to freeze at the end of the week, this could prevent us from having to do IVF in future.

As long as we have embryos in the freezer we would only ever need an embryo transfer, meaning if this cycle doesn't work or if it does and we decide to try for a sibling, we would start the process from here, where we are today, bypassing everything prior to this as our embryo would already be created and ready for us to transfer. This also means we only have to pay for transfer, rather than full IVF, although we'll have to pay freezer storage monthly for any embryos. Another benefit of embryo transfer over IVF is that there's nowhere near as many drugs or injections.

We still wouldn't have any guarantees, our embryos would still have to survive the freeze and subsequent thaw, we'd still need a successful implantation etc. but for now numbers offered hope.

From such a hope-deprived diagnosis to a feeling of reproductive destitution, I was absolutely holding on to any tiny glimmer of hope I could, holding on so goddamn tight that my fingertips were white with desperation.

I'm getting used to the pessaries now, a few practices and I seemed to get the hang of it. I realised that if I keep my finger on the release button, even as I remove the applicator rather than pressing it, releasing it and then removing the applicator, it seems to work.

The leaking I was warned about is minimal, barely any to be honest.

So I now eagerly await "conception".

Tomorrow I will technically be pregnant, or PUPO as "we" call it…

Pregnant Until Proven Otherwise.

24/08/2019

Transfer

I'M PREGNANT!!! (technically)

ARRRGGGHHHHHH!!!

I can't quite believe we've come so far, we've done it – I just need to stay pregnant, but for now I am PUPO.

Transfer itself (yesterday) was amazing, we watched on the ultrasound screen and saw the embryo being inserted. It looks like a flash of light and then you're left with a little, bright white "splodge".

The embryologist gave us a picture of the specific embryo she had chosen which was really lovely.

The procedure itself is absolutely fine, you barely feel anything, in fact the worst part is having a full bladder and a sonographer pushing on your tummy to scan the procedure. It's similar to my experience of a smear test (with the addition of the scan).

We were advised that if the embryo is strong enough to attach then it will and if it isn't then it won't. I was so thankful for these words as it takes away the burden of responsibility I had been dreading.

The good news didn't end there, we currently have 4 embryos to freeze; the 5th one still has a little more time to get to the required stage for freezing so the embryologist is going to call later today with a final update but we definitely have 4 which is odd-defying and amazing.

Although what would seem like such a happy part of the process, it appears that, particularly for me, the emotional aspect of the whole thing comes to a head and right around transfer comes the crash.

You see, it makes sense really – throughout treatment you are climbing up, up and up, building your high with each day that passes and each milestone is reached that eventually you're at such a peak that it doesn't take much and you fall and obviously the higher the buzz, the further you have to fall and I have absolutely crashed. I'm an emotional mess. I feel unexplainably sad, relieved, excited, quite the contradictory cocktail.

Steve and I were always quite pleasantly surprised at how well I'd handled the emotional aspect of treatment, being that I am an emotional person anyway.

I guess for the past few weeks I have suppressed any severe emotion as much as possible without being unhealthy, to allow focus and clarity on treatment itself, meaning that this crash is actually 4 weeks' worth. I'm aware that the emotional stress on my body can't be a good thing considering I am PUPO, so I really need to work out of this "low" and try to hold onto the positives I have been blessed with.

We are in such an amazing position and this cycle has been one that has impressed even the professionals at the clinic. We have a lot to be happy about and I know that this crash will soon subside.

Let's also not forget the fact…

I'M PREGNANT!!!!!

Now for the 2-week wait!

03/09/2019

The two-week wait

Over halfway through the dreaded two-week wait and I must admit I'm doing so much better emotionally than what I had expected, it hasn't been too bad.

The first week flew by; it helped that Steve was off work and we had his daughter for the majority of the week, meaning we had no choice but to keep busy. These last few days are starting to drag and my excitement exhausts me at times, but considering test day is now only two full days away, I'm pleasantly surprised at how quickly it has come around.

I'd expected to really struggle and although I have felt a little hormonal it hasn't necessarily been due to the wait which I thought it would be.

Hormones are a wonderful thing and following my transfer I felt typical period-like symptoms, teary etc. The fact that I now have excitement building allows for this hormonal imbalance to appear somewhat less unpleasant. I'll tell you something that is unpleasant that I hadn't even considered during the two-week wait – my physical state. I thought my body would be well into recovery by this stage.

Honestly, sometimes I struggle to move, I feel like my abs have had the workout of a lifetime (although unless that workout was eating, it sure doesn't look like it). I've got period-like cramps constantly, literally my whole abdomen feels as if it is being stretched. I had no idea it would feel this sore at this stage. Everything I've read, including the info the clinic send you away with, say cramping is totally normal and if I'm honest I do feel like a bit of a wuss, but this is bad.

My fear is, I already feel unable to complain.

I chose this and I fought so desperately to get pregnant, I can imagine people's insensitivity to any suffering I may voice throughout pregnancy. I chose to be pregnant, not to be in pain, similar to the fact I agreed to do IVF but I didn't choose the unpleasant side effects. We'll see how things go anyway.

Countdown for the weekend is on.

Test day is on Friday – although we have a family wedding on Saturday and it's not far from my house, meaning my Mum, Auntie Kerry and Granny Anny are coming to my house beforehand. Now they've been told a bit of a fib; that test day is Monday (we told them that the test is just over two weeks after transfer). I want the enjoyment and shock when we tell them (hopefully good news) and I knew that if they knew test day was Friday there's no way they'd wait until Saturday to hear the news, and I certainly am not telling them over the phone, so the plan is to test Friday and tell them face to face on Saturday, when they won't expect it.

Apart from, of course, Steve's parents, these are the only family members we are telling straight away, everyone else will be told at the 3-month mark.

I'm so excited, I swear I am pregnant, I just have this feeling.

Considering the horror stories I read about the 2-week wait, I'm really genuinely amazed at how we've just got on with things.

I guess that sums up our IVF journey to be honest, looking back it absolutely was not as bad as I'd imagined; don't get me wrong – it sucks! I'd rather not have had to go through it, obviously and I'm not taking anything away from anyone that may suffer more than I did, but for me, it was manageable, we just got on with it.

Maybe I'd feel differently if we hadn't have had such great numbers or maybe I'll feel differently if we don't get good news on Friday, I guess it's much easier to look back on a journey of success with positivity.

Regardless of the outcome – YOU CAN DO IT!

The pain caused by the desperation to be a parent is far greater than any physical aspect of IVF.

TRIGGER WARNING

Please note there is reference to pregnancy and birth throughout the rest of this book.

06/09/2019

The Test

IT'S POSITIVE!!!

ARRRGGGHHHHH!!!

First of all, I have to admit, we did cheat a little, and we tested last night.

I had been so cool and relaxed about the two-week wait and I hadn't even considered testing early, until yesterday. Suddenly it pecked away at me all day, I spoke to Steve and we both agreed, what difference would 10/11 hours make? I was still nervous about early testing but not enough to stop me from doing it.

I literally sat at the window waiting for Steve to get home from work. We wanted to do it together and he was bringing home extra tests so I could still do the official clinic test in the morning as instructed. He'd barely walked through the front door and I'd snatched the box off him and ran upstairs.

As we waited, I was filled with an unbelievable rush of excitement. I could tell Steve was nervous; he doesn't often give much away but this was written all over his face.

Steve offered to look, but knowing the joker he was, I was unsure if that was what I wanted. Would he really joke about something like this?

As he picked up the test I knew... His smile of relief gave him away instantly and I grabbed him into a cuddle and I burst into tears...

WE'RE HAVING A BABY!!!

Steve immediately took to the protective Daddy role and instructed how I must remain calm and stress free, I have to take it easy and not let anything stress me out, and I loved this side of him.

We went straight up to Steve's parents house to share the news. I had to tell someone, I felt like I could burst. I thought I'd have blurted it out as soon as we walked through the door but Steve's dad was pottering in the garage and naturally Steve joined him. I really struggled to make small talk with Steve's mum, whilst waiting for the boys. I was so aware of my facial expressions, I desperately didn't want to give anything away without Steve being there.

Finally we could tell them, we were all together and I let Steve take the lead.

They were as full of joy as expected, it was truly lovely, I have no idea how I held it together to be honest.

The evening was naturally full of baby talk and I couldn't help but feel my heart was finally full.

I slept restlessly, the adrenaline and excitement would not allow me to rest.

Steve woke me this morning when his alarm went off for work. I did the test that the clinic had provided and it confirmed our news. I feel like I'm in a bubble. A bubble of joy that no one can pop. And I absolutely can't wait for tomorrow when I can tell "my lot".

According to Google I am now 4 weeks pregnant – I had always assumed that at this point I'd be 2 weeks pregnant. I had to call the clinic at 9AM anyway so I could ask them roughly how far along I am.

I can't believe it's worked and I am saying these words:

WE'RE HAVING A BABY!!!

09/09/2019

Rice Rice Baby

Telling my family was amazing, everything I wanted it to be. They're overjoyed for us but also somewhat reserved. The 12-week mark will allow for a more relaxed celebration.

The wedding on the Saturday evening was a welcome change of scenery and allowed a sense of fun I wasn't expecting. I struggled to contain my new secret, I've waited so long for this and I just wanted to share my happiness with everyone.

I also feel excitedly reserved, I've never been a reserved person so the fact I have such a precious secret that can't yet be revealed means I'm a little more withdrawn than usual. Purely out of fear that my excitement might slip and give me away.

I'm feeling more and more tired as each day passes but at 5 weeks pregnant that's normal.

YES – You read that right – 5 weeks pregnant!

The clinic confirmed all of this when I called on Friday to give them our test results.

Any "normal" pregnancy is counted from the date of your last period, an IVF pregnancy is no different – meaning I am now 5 weeks pregnant.

We have our first scan booked for 25th September, making this dream feel a little more real.

Naturally I am now more baby mad than ever, I downloaded a baby app immediately following the test and have looked at it about 10 times a day ever since.

At 5 weeks pregnant our baby is the size of a grain of rice. A little speckle of preciousness.

Steve and I have discussed everything, from prams to car seats, from nursery to baby swimming lessons; the excitement won't allow me to chill. We even had a sneaky look at prams in a baby shop on Sunday.

Heartburn is a killer, one I am more than prepared to put up with I can assure you, but unpleasant all the same.

According to all of my reading, my symptoms are all normal.

After IVF, I'd pretty much put up with anything to get our little splodge from a grain of rice to a baby.

13/09/2019

Mum's the word

I had a meeting with work this week; it went well but I didn't expect anything less to be honest.

Steve and I had already agreed that I would immediately inform HR as soon as we knew.

My previous lengthy absence had caused some anxiety regarding work. Naturally my defences were up and have been since December. Luckily my contract means I get school holidays off so I hadn't had to worry about work through IVF as it has all taken place during the summer holidays.

I was absent from work for the first two weeks of September, for my two-week wait. Many people will see this differently and I know some will see work as a welcome distraction, but there's no way I could have worked through it – my stress capacity was already full to the brim with fertility, I had absolutely zero tolerance for work as well.

As soon as we had the news I emailed work to arrange a meeting. I didn't want to wait until my current sick note ran out or until they contacted me; I wanted to regain a little control again and I had no reason to hide away.

Needless to say the positive test and the relief of successfully completing IVF had me in such a good head space that I felt it was the right time to face the things I had shut away. The fact I also knew I was now legally protected at work also allowed for some extra back up in aiding my positive attitude.

I suggested a return to work for the upcoming Monday – pregnant women work full time and apart from early pregnancy symptoms there wasn't anything wrong with me. I'm actually looking forward to returning to some kind of normality.

Everyone I saw in work asked how I was, I'd always been so open about my infertility so many knew I'd been doing IVF over summer and they were keen for updates. I found it easier than expected repeating the same cover story. Ever more exciting knowing I was growing my own little secret.

A part of me feels somewhat anxious about the fact I am lying to people, people that care about me and take the time to ask for updates, but I'm pretty sure, they'll understand when we do announce.

16/09/2019

Double Trouble

Steve's daughter had a dance show on Saturday and I'd been looking forward to it for months. I'd felt slight period-like cramps all afternoon on Saturday but didn't think much of it. I didn't even mention it to Steve as I just assumed it was normal.

NEVER ASSUME!

Don't feel silly, always check everything that doesn't feel normal to you.

At around 5:30pm, as we were getting ready to leave, I went to the toilet and noticed blood, far more than I felt comfortable with. The feeling of dread and panic instantly pulsated through my body. Steve and I took to Google hoping to see something reassuring. As many things scared us as they did reassure us, and I was left feeling even more confused.

I was certain the bleeding had stopped, a few wipes and the tissue appeared free of blood so we decided to head to the show and keep our eye on it.

I must have gone to the toilet about 5 times in the 45 minutes we were there, desperately hoping that I didn't see any blood. If the clinic had been open I would have called them straight away but with it being a weekend our only option was A&E and I really didn't want to make a fuss.

Please take my advice and fuss away.

A part of me was also avoiding seeking medical attention in the hope that the dread would just go away – it doesn't.

As people arrived for the show and spoke to us, all I could think about was what was potentially happening to me and our baby. I couldn't make or hold a conversation as my concentration was focused elsewhere – totally consumed with panic.

When Steve's mum and dad arrived at the show we quietly advised Steve's mum that we were going to A&E – the 5 more trips to the toilet had only further confirmed our dread and we asked Steve's mum to make excuses for us.

People were aware I had recently done IVF so she just said I wasn't feeling very well.

After what felt like hours we were finally seen by a Doctor and he advised that I was being admitted to the Gynaecology ward. Once admitted we were seen by the specialist Doctor immediately.

He advised that he needed to do a blood test to confirm my HCG level was above 1500. If it was then this would be a good sign and we would have a scan in the morning. If my HCG level was below 1500 we would have to wait 48 hours and do a repeat blood test to see if my HCG level was rising, then we would have a scan.

HCG should continually rise when pregnant so he explained this is what he was looking for. He also wanted to complete an internal examination to confirm if my cervix was closed. This would indicate that I was still pregnant and baby was safe.

Internal examinations are never pleasant, much like a smear test to be honest, but the speculum seemed more uncomfortable than usual. He couldn't find my cervix, which was neither good nor bad, but he advised that he couldn't see any active bleeding which was a really positive sign.

As it was now late on Saturday night, or rather early on Sunday morning and the blood test would take some hours to come back from the lab, the doctor advised us to go home. He said he would call us at 7am with the blood results and advise us of the next steps. Needless to say I hardly slept but the bleeding had stopped which offered a little hope.

The 7am call came and offered the much needed relief we were so desperate for. My HCG was over 9000 and I was booked for a scan at 10:50am. Following the scan I was to return to the ward to debrief with the Doctor.

The scan filled me with excitement – I was going to see our baby for the first time. Steve came into the room with me as we didn't want him to miss anything.

The sonographer struggled to see anything initially which really scared us but she explained that my ovaries were still so large from IVF that they were covering everything else. She mentioned hyperstimulation and immediately I thought of our cover story – how ironic that our fib of a cover story may now have some truth – serves us right.

She decided an internal scan would be better but I was worried: would this be harmful to our baby?

She explained that she wasn't really going anywhere near baby so there was no need to worry.

As the sonographer fiddled with the scan probe she said "Were you expecting a twin pregnancy?" Steve and I immediately looked at each other and I could see the excitement in his eyes.

She explained how she could see 2 sacs but only 1 heartbeat; the excitement for possible twins was dashed within seconds and I felt so sorry for Steve.

The sonographer showed us our baby and we even got to see the heartbeat; it was so tiny but so very special. A moment I will honestly never forget and a feeling of such intense relief I just wanted to cry.

When we returned to the ward and saw the Doctor, he explained that the second sac could be one of two things: either a possible twin pregnancy that hasn't quite developed properly or a haemorrhage. Either of these things could explain the bleeding and whichever one of these things that it was, there was no way of knowing for sure. I was thankful in a way as not knowing meant I didn't feel the sadness or grief I maybe would have. The Doctor was happy that the second sac, whatever it was, wasn't putting our baby at risk and my body would absorb whatever was left of it.

PHEWWWWW!

I obviously couldn't have been more thankful that our baby was safe. It surprised me how protective I already felt for this tiny little splodge.

I now just wanted my bed, I hadn't slept much and I just wanted to snuggle up with my little splodge knowing he/she was safe and well.

This morning I called the clinic, just to advise them of the weekend's events. I had spoken to work via text yesterday afternoon to advise them I wouldn't be in today. I needed to update the clinic and I wasn't sure if they'd need to see me etc.

The clinic confirmed we had definitely done the right thing, they want to leave my 7 week scan as it is and they have updated my file.

So back to work and some form of normality tomorrow.

I can safely say the heartburn has returned, although I'm thankful for the reminder that splodge is well and truly ok.

06/10/2019

Check-In

So… I haven't written in here for a few weeks now and a lot has been happening…

We've had scans, midwife appointments, pregnancy symptoms; truth is, I've been enjoying pregnancy, I have waited years to feel like this and it's truly amazing.

Our scan at the private clinic was perfect, Baby N is doing well and the second sac we had previously seen has almost gone, meaning it was most likely a haemorrhage than anything else. I spotted a few times (random bleeding) following our first scare but have now been bleed free for over a week so hopefully that's the end of that. The clinic confirmed Baby N is growing perfectly, so much so that they have discharged us and handed us back to the NHS for routine monitoring.

Our first midwife appointment, last week, also went well – lots of paperwork as is the norm for your first appointment but it's all starting to feel more and more real.

I even got my green book from the midwife. The green book is significant as not only does it confirm your pregnancy but it is now my bible. I have to take it to every appointment etc. It's my certificate of pregnancy.

And if the appointments hadn't made this all feel real then the symptoms sure did.

No real sickness yet, certainly not the daily sickness so commonly associated with pregnancy, but heartburn and headaches and a queasy feeling have wiped me out this past week. The over-riding symptom is most definitely fatigue; I mean, I slept a lot anyway, I cannot function properly on less than 8 hours but this is different… I am literally exhausted all the time, as if I'm never fully awake.

I'm conscious not to complain, I am genuinely loving every second and feel truly blessed to be experiencing such a miracle. These symptoms are bittersweet; although they are unpleasant they act as a constant reminder of what we have achieved and how far we have come – I'm finally pregnant.

I'm still massive, the clinic confirmed both my ovaries are still enlarged which is completely normal after IVF. I already have a bump which makes keeping the secret even harder. We just keep blaming IVF bloat.

As my ovaries reduce in size and baby grows, I should eventually "even out". I won't really notice an increase in size like you normally would until around 12/13 weeks, as I am already so big now.

My sense of smell is heightened beyond belief, it's crazy that something the size of a grape can do such drastic things to your body and your senses.

Baby N does NOT like bread and butter, the thought of it makes me feel genuinely sick. I remember dipping some bread into some soup recently and thinking the butter had gone bad, it tasted sour like yoghurt.

All pregnancies are different but I'm so excited to share mine; for now the secret is still shared only with a select few – we are 3 weeks away from announcing, my scan is booked for 31st October – Halloween – Yikes!

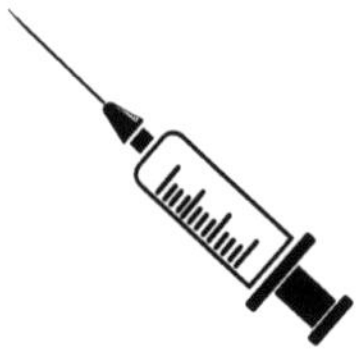

26/10/2019

Pregnancy Rage

Don't get me wrong, I am happy. So happy. But I could also rip someone's head off at any given second.

I haven't been as emotional as I expected, with hormones all over the place it is common to experience mood swings, particularly during the first trimester. Considering I am an emotional person anyway I had expected this to intensify during pregnancy, but I just feel pissed off, at everyone, for everything. My patience is almost non-existent and I can't count the amount of times I've apologised to Steve when actually I just want to cave his head in.

It saddens me a little that my temper won't allow me to express my happiness. I'm also conscious that it may come across like I am miserable; truth is I am so overjoyed.

Symptom-wise I am so lucky, barely any sickness although I have often felt queasy. I'm still so tired –

maybe this is a contributing factor to the building rage?

I've found the first trimester more difficult because I am filled with excitement but the few that do know are still somewhat reserved. I know why it is this way but it's still really sad that people don't seem as happy as I am. Steve being one of these people that I unfortunately can't share my excitement with, he's very much waiting for the 12 week mark before celebrating.

I'm holding out for next week's appointment, after which we are telling Steve's daughter. I'm hoping this will raise his spirits and allow him to relax a little more and enjoy this with me.

08/11/2019

The secret is out

Finally!!!!!

It has been wonderful sharing our news with the people we love.

Steve's daughter didn't quite realise at first – we had set up a hunt all around the house, a "guess who" hunt…

1. Time for a game, it's called "guess who?" – to get it right you must solve the clues. One by one you must guess who I am, the first one is easy, it's in Daddy's van.

2. Am I a dog? Or am I a cat? You won't find me inside a hat. Am I bald or do I have hair? For your next clue you'll need to look under the stairs.

3. Another clue, try not to peep, your next clue is where Daddy and Jodie sleep.

4. For this next one, you may need to go far, it's hiding in the boot of the car.

5. Do I bark? Or meow? Or talk? Your next clue can be found where you keep the forks.

6. Now look outside and search a lot, it's hiding in a flower pot.

7. It that all the clues? Oh no it's not… The next one is hiding in a place that gets hot.

8. Have you sussed it? How many clues have you found? Your final one is in the lounge.

9. I can't wait to meet you and be best friends, I'm super excited, let the fun begin. I'm not ready yet, I'm coming in May but I already love you more than words can say. So can you guess? Am I a Miss or a Mr? No-one knows yet – I'm your new baby brother or sister!

It took a few moments for the news to register but when it did, by gosh was she excited.

Sharing our news has also come as a reminder that this is a much bigger deal to us than many. Don't get me wrong, people are quite obviously happy for us but some people's congratulations seem somewhat under-whelming – maybe it's me, I just feel like some don't get it.

Aside from the under-whelming celebrations we've had an amazing pregnancy so far. Our scan last week was such a gorgeous experience, the first time Baby N actually looked like a baby rather than a splodge.

It's nice to just be open and relaxed rather than having to hide everything and think about what I can say to who, not to mention I most definitely have a baby bump so it's a good job I don't have to hide it anymore. Steve is becoming more excited too which is nice to see, he's very practical so wants to get the nursery sorted ASAP, which is fine with me, but I want to really enjoy these experiences and not rush them.

We've decided not to officially announce on social media just yet, we know all too well how it feels to be on the other side of those announcements and considering how open I was about my IVF struggle I desperately don't want to appear as if I'm gloating now and undermine the very real struggle we faced. It isn't a secret though and I have individually messaged those people who reached out to me during IVF whom I want to share the news with.

Many friends have encouraged me to share our news, even in social media, some think that my good news will offer hope rather than sadness; however, having been on the receiving end of such news before, I'm still not sure; maybe I will change my mind further down the line? If someone was to put something about my pregnancy on social media I wouldn't rush to delete it or hide it and I guess as pictures are uploaded of me, people will soon start to realise.

It still doesn't feel real, I can't believe we did it. It baffles me that I have a tiny human growing in my tummy, symptoms are absolutely real but it amazes me to think this is it… I'm going to be a Mummy.

27/11/2019

Wee'ly Funny

I feel like I've neglected my book recently and I feel rather guilty about it, as if some form of betrayal to this object that has offered so much support to me throughout my journey. It really has been my ultimate companion over the past 12 months and got me through some of my most difficult times.

Now those times have been replaced by happier moments, moments of pregnancy, and I feel my book has been somewhat replaced with enjoying these new experiences, as if my book is now more of an after-thought rather than my go-to. I don't need the daily escape the book used to offer.

That being said, I'm not ready to completely part with it yet, I'm convinced my story will naturally come to an end and right now doesn't feel like that time. I still have far too much to share.

I've felt Baby N move for the first time recently – what an amazing experience that is. I couldn't be sure at first, the fluttering sensation was so delicate and I had become so used to listening to my body through IVF that it could have been anything to be honest. The Midwife confirmed it was Baby N at our recent appointment. We heard Baby N's heartbeat for the first time, another wonderfully beautiful moment. Although we'd seen the tiny flicker of the heartbeat on the screen previously, there's nothing quite like hearing it for the first time. Our Midwife had said she could feel Baby N kicking against the Doppler probe, confirming my recent flutters are most likely signs of a very active baby. It's extremely exciting.

Steve and I seem to be in an amazing place right now which is also lovely, I guess the stress of everything we've been through finally subsiding has allowed us to have fun again. I must admit I seem to be laughing so much recently. Dangerous when pregnant…

Yes I have wee'd!

No not intentionally!

Yes by accident!

No I'm not kidding.

It does feel good to enjoy laughing with Steve again. Don't misunderstand – there are still times when I want to punch him in the face, but he usually makes a joke out of it which makes me laugh, which then makes me wee, by which point I've forgotten that I was ever mad at him and we are both in fits of giggles at my blatant lack of bladder control.

I'm embracing every second – even the part where I wee myself.

21/01/2020

Oh Boy! It's A Girl

WE'RE HAVING A GIRL!!!!!!!

It's starting to feel more and more real as each day passes.

Knowing the gender of my baby has really helped confirm the realness of my pregnancy and I instantly felt connected to her.

I'm now 24 weeks pregnant and movements are much more frequent and incredibly strong. It really does feel amazing and I truly cherish every flutter, even the 5am drum practice on my bladder.

Now as amazing as all of this sounds and it really is, there's also a darker side to pregnancy for some that we don't often talk about, for many reasons; pregnancy depression is very real and can be such a struggle for many, it's so confusing and scary and I want to continue to share everything with you, in the hope that you don't ever feel alone.

It's real and it's OK!

I think the hardest and most confusing thing for me is that I am happy, I am genuinely overjoyed at such a blessing and I am excited to meet my new best friend, so feeling teary and sad for some unknown reason just doesn't seem to match how I think I feel. The confusion adds to the stress and makes me feel so frustrated with myself. Why can't I just enjoy this? I've waited so long and fought so hard and now I have everything I ever wanted so why can't I just be happy?

With all of this comes an incredible amount of guilt: I'm so very lucky and yet I'm wallowing which only makes me even more frustrated. It becomes so exhausting that I am overcome with tiredness and emotions and I seem to cry uncontrollably, I'm then very aware of what this is doing to this little life growing inside me and BAM – there's that guilt again.

Initially I put it down to hormones – we hear a lot about how hormones and emotions are intensified during pregnancy and I thought it must just be my body's way of dealing with the changes. My advice would be – you know your body! If something isn't right or feels slightly off please talk about it, don't try to find excuses or shrug it off, just mention it to someone. It may well be hormones and if it is then talking your feelings through with someone won't hurt and may be a good release for you, but if it is something a little more serious then help isn't something you should be depriving yourself of.

It was actually Steve who noticed how serious this was and pointed it out to me. I had a bit of an emotional breakdown over Christmas and Steve really tried, as usual, to say all the right things and comfort me. Little did I know, he'd been Googling my symptoms for a few days and he eventually sat me down and explained that he was concerned that maybe I was suffering with something called pregnancy depression; he asked me how I felt about it and we discussed the symptoms. Steve suggested I book an appointment with the GP and offered to come with me. I broke down. Relief, I think. I wasn't going mad and maybe there was something we could do. I called my GP straight away who agreed to see me that same day.

The GP confirmed I was experiencing pregnancy depression and referred me for some talking therapy. We did discuss medication and although there are no direct links to any risks during pregnancy I chose to decline medication, for now. I have experienced depression before and talking therapy really helped me; ideally if we can manage this episode with talking therapy and avoid medication this would be preferred.

I have my first session in 2 weeks and I am hopeful. It's an instant relief to know there is a reason for feeling this way – I can stop questioning myself.

I have chosen for the time being, to only share this diagnosis with a select few. Rightly or wrongly I do feel like people will judge me, I mean, I judged myself to begin with so why wouldn't others? It's easy to feel like people won't understand and I've decided I don't want to show any more vulnerability. Steve and I are on the right path and we will deal with this together for now.

I'm so very grateful for the care and protection he has shown me. Considering he admittedly doesn't understand mental health, he's been amazing and continues to be.

But don't tell him I said that…

I am very much still enjoying pregnancy, the physical symptoms are sometimes hard but on the whole I've been very lucky, pregnancy has been kind to me.

Struggling emotionally doesn't mean I don't enjoy the experience, my pregnancy is no less magical – even the pelvic girdle pain and Braxton Hicks – oh how magical!...

12/04/2020

Far Cough COVID

It's been a while, and boy has a lot happened…

Talking therapy really helped, I've completed my course and to be honest, compared to how I felt, I'm confident the worst has passed. I'm still hormonal but not as sad or teary.

Pregnancy rage has returned with vengeance, pretty sure Steve thinks this is now my "normal" state.

The closer we get to due date the more excited Steve seems to be, he hasn't really been too interested in the movements, it kind of freaks him out when he sees or feels my tummy move – which surprises me and to be honest I did find this a little disappointing in the beginning. I wanted to share the magic of baby movements with him. He shows willing for my sake, but I know he's not a fan.

My recent midwife appointment confirmed everything is on track and both Baby N and I are showing signs that we are readying for her arrival. I have been advised to use my birthing ball (like a space hopper for grown-ups) – this should hopefully open my pelvis and allow Baby N to engage. Steve is now the official space hopper monitor, much to my annoyance – every day, he calls me from work "Are you on that ball?" – he's so excited, he just wants her here. I'm in two minds, to be honest… Of course I want her here but I've loved being pregnant and I really don't want to wish away these last 4 weeks.

Although… with the current COVID situation, wishing away time is something I think we all wish we had the power to do.

I don't need to tell you what COVID is, it's a worldwide pandemic, I'm sure you're all aware… Something I'm not sure everyone is aware of though, is the effect this has on pregnancy and labour.

Social distancing has completely thrown my birth plan out of the window, not to mention the fact that I feel robbed of the last 4 weeks of my pregnancy. No visitors, no antenatal classes, no breastfeeding support, I really am going into this blind and I feel absolutely alone.

I see my Midwife once every 2 weeks but that's it as far as support.

Labour also looks very different for us too. Steve can be present for active labour only (from 4cm dilated) and can only stay for birth, meaning if I am kept in hospital or moved to a ward following birth, he will be asked to leave and won't see me or our baby until we are discharged. He's as laid back as ever but if he misses the beginning of his baby's life, I will be heartbroken.

I will also have to undergo any pre-labour procedures alone, so any sweeps or induction I will have to do without him, which terrifies me.

I'm due induction on my due date, if we don't have any signs by then, so the professionals are keen for an early arrival. Hopefully if she gets a wriggle on before due date and I am discharged fairly quickly then the only change for us will be that my mum won't be there (1 birthing partner only) and the fact we won't have any visitors or be able to introduce her to the world.

It's such a scary time, I know why these measures have been put into place and of course we want her here safe more than anything else. I just can't help but feel so frustrated at this whole thing…

Six years of trying to conceive, a round of self-funded IVF, only to be facing labour during a worldwide pandemic, I mean COME ON!!!!

That sickly sweet cocktail I thought I'd gotten rid of once and for all has been served yet again, only this time it's a double, and it hasn't been placed in front of me with a neatly folded napkin…

NO!

It's been thrown at me, splash in the face like a bitch slap I never saw coming.

Eviction Notice

In the run up to due date I was so desperate to get her here that every single twinge or pain I set my timer in the hope of a pattern so I could claim them as contractions. The closer we got to due date the more the panic set in, as I was faced with the possibility of having to go through some of the labour process alone.

I'd been booked sweeps at 38 weeks and 39 weeks and then induction on due date. Due to this awful COVID situation, Steve was unable to attend any of these procedures with me, and would only be allowed to join me once I was 4cm dilated as this was classed as active labour. Inductions can sometimes take days and you can also be admitted overnight – the thought of Steve missing anything absolutely broke my heart; it also filled me with fear.

We were so desperate for an early arrival, we tried everything: curry, walk, birthing ball, bath, clary sage oil, and raspberry leaf tea, everything... yes, even that!!!!!

Not fun, or romantic, more of a job that needed doing.

We laughed the whole way through which didn't help, nor did the fact I was the size of a house.

Nothing worked and the saddest part was I spent the final few weeks of pregnancy scared and annoyed and wishing pregnancy would hurry up and progress to birth. I imagine most mums become inpatient towards the end, excited and desperate to meet their little ones. I just wish mine wasn't tinged with panic and fear, an all too familiar cocktail.

Labour Day

My birthing plan had to be somewhat amended due to COVID restrictions and I was gutted I couldn't have both my mum and Steve as originally planned; however, I was thankful that having Steve for at least some of the process was still an option.

The main points of my birthing plan, that hadn't changed were: I don't like needles and I don't want an epidural if I could help it, although I wasn't against it if absolutely necessary.

The sweep at 38 weeks had been unsuccessful, my cervix was too low and too far back meaning it couldn't be reached properly by the midwife. She did what she could but it didn't work so I was back for another sweep at 39 weeks.

This sweep was successful, in the fact that all signs looked good for labour to start soon and my cervix was in a position that meant that the midwife could do what she needed to do.

My god did she stretch that cervix… Christ, I was nearly on the ceiling.

After having both an unsuccessful and successful sweep, let me tell you they are not pleasant, but I was keen for it to work –, I mean, I'm there anyway, with it all hanging out, so may as well make it work it – don't be gentle, just get it done!

Unfortunately even with all the positive signs, Baby N seemed far too comfortable and the sweeps didn't work.

Monday 11th May (due date) 9am I was booked for induction. I knew I was already 2cm dilated as I'd been advised at my 39 week sweep.

Steve waited outside the hospital for any updates I could provide via text – once we knew what was actually happening, he could decide whether to wait or go home. I was advised my cervix was very favourable for labour.

Induction is used to help the cervix when this is not the case, so there wasn't much point in putting me through the balloon and/or pessary induction because technically I was already at the stage that these procedures are designed to achieve. What they could do and agreed to do for me was break my waters.

So home we went awaiting a call for the labour ward when they were ready for us.

We got the call – Tuesday 12th May 3pm, I was to attend labour ward to have my waters broken and labour started.

Because my waters were broken manually, I was automatically put on a hormone drip to start contractions straight away – the hope is that labour will start very quickly and because of this the lead midwife agreed Steve could join me to have my waters broken rather than making us wait and me being alone until I reached 4cm; we were so thankful for this.

My waters were broken at 4pm and the drip was started at 4:30pm. Having my waters broken was completely painless, just felt like I'd wet myself, a feeling I was familiar with. I hadn't quite imagined there to be so much fluid and I thought it would all come at once, but you think it's all out and then you move position and even more comes out, it never seemed to end. I felt dirty and sticky and obviously wet, I just wanted to shower and feel clean, but I had a feeling this was probably the cleanest I would feel for a while, things were about to get a little messier...

The drip increases in dosage until you reach a level that starts contractions; it's different for everyone so some may react straight away and some can require a high dose to get them started.

The drip dosage doubles every half hour and I reacted as follows:

4:30pm – 1ml

5pm – 2ml

5:30pm – 4ml

6pm – 8ml

OH SHIT!!!

HELLO CONTRACTIONS!!!

Now I don't know if the drip causes more painful contractions, I've heard that it can and the midwife said that artificial processes, particularly drug induced, tend to be stronger than natural processes. Like I said, I don't know as I've never had natural contractions to compare this to, but I found it went from nothing to everything in one breath, out of nowhere they just came. There wasn't a build-up or a chance for my body to get used to the sensation, or to adapt as the contractions grew from mild to moderate then severe, there wasn't a gradual increase over a period of time, I just found myself thinking OH SHIT! Full force, they were here.

Ideally, contractions should be 3 or 4 every 10 minutes, mine started straight away 5 or 6 every 10 minutes. At this stage it just meant 4ml wasn't enough and 8ml was too much, so they switched the drip off to see if my contractions slowed – plan being that if they did I could go back on the drip at a more tailored dose.

8pm and I was still 5/6 every 10 minutes, lasting approximately 45 seconds each. I needed gas and air at this stage, I just couldn't tolerate it anymore, I felt like they were now way more intense than before and I couldn't manage. My contractions were right down in my bum and at their peak I couldn't help kicking my legs about, literally as if I was having a fit, I couldn't control it, they just kicked out.

The difficulty with my contractions was there was no rest period – just as one was coming down and I had started to catch my breath, the next one had already started.

8:30pm and I was still 5/6 every 10 minutes. I was given an injection to reverse the effects of the drip, the injection should totally cancel the drip out, as if I'd never had it.

9pm and I was still 5/6 every 10 minutes, I was given another injection (you can only ever have 2 of these injections).

I was due an examination at 10PM to see how far dilated I was.

9:30pm/9:45pm I was in agony, still all in my bum and I felt like I needed to push, I didn't know what I needed to push? A poo? A baby? But I really needed to push this feeling out of my bum – "it" was right there, and I just needed "it" gone. By "it" I think I mean the pain but "pain" seems such an inferior word to use to describe something so horrendous that I'd rather shit in my own hands and clap than experience this sensation ever again. In a panic I shouted to Steve "I need to push", ironic really because his face looked like I had actually just shit in my hands and clapped. He went to get the midwife who came to examine me.

Baby N was back to back – typical, considering she'd been in the perfect position for labour for weeks, and at the last moment she'd turned herself into the most awkward position possible. This explained why I had so much pain down in my bum.

"OK so that makes sense, how dilated am I?"

2 BLOODY CM!!!

I'd been 2 cm all bloody week, since my sweep.

2 BLOODY CM!!!

Not having it, your fingers are wrong.

2 BLOODY CM!!!

What the hell am I going to do? She's going to be stuck up there forever.

2 BLOODY CM!!!

2 BLOODY CM!!!!!!!!!!!!!

The Consultant came to see us and have a chat with us about our options, of which there weren't many.

We needed labour to progress and dilate my cervix and if my body is struggling to do that the drip is required to assist; we can't use the drip because I'm contracting too often (still 5/6 every 10 minutes), basically my body was working too hard on the frequency and not enough on progression/dilation.

We were stuck at a standstill. A very painful standstill.

All I knew was that I'd been at this for 4/5 hours for pretty much nothing and the pain was unbearable – what happens if I go another 10 hours?

I started to panic.

Everyone (consultant/midwife/Steve) suggested an epidural, but I was petrified.

Obviously my fear of needles meant I'd rather avoid one at all costs, not to mention the scary stories you hear about how they can paralyse you, not a great advertisement either, nor was having a cannula like tube threaded into my spine all whilst having to remain incredibly still, whilst bent forward, hugging a 40 week baby bump, not forgetting that my coping mechanism for a contraction was to spontaneously, uncontrollably, kick out my legs.

On the other hand, I knew I couldn't carry on like this.

Let's try for a little longer and see if I progress.

Midnight – 6-7 hours of induced contractions causing hellish pain, still 5/6 every 10 minutes, trying to avoid that goddamn epidural.

I gave in!

I couldn't do it!

I needed the epidural!

I was gutted!

I wanted to be brave and strong and I felt like I'd copped out, what a wuss!

Two things swung it for me – 1 being that the anaesthetist explained that this isn't an endurance challenge, if we can do something to make me more comfortable then why wouldn't we? The other thing that swung it for me was both Steve and I said if I had the epidural then that's the worst that this is ever going to be, however long labour took it'd be pain free as I'd be numb from the epidural and god forbid I ended up having to have a C-Section, the epidural would have already have been inserted.

The thought of getting through this one thing and then labour and birth could only get better from then on, won me over.

Half an hour later and I was literally so annoyed with myself.

Why the hell didn't I do this sooner?

This is amazing!

Having it done wasn't even that bad, yes I had to really concentrate and yes the local anaesthetic bloody hurt but it was manageable, way more manageable than those contractions. So I'd tolerated 6 hours of hell for nothing, out of fear for something that I ended up having anyway and it wasn't even that bad.

What a knob!

Contractions continued, 5/6 every 10 minutes and the consultant came back to see us. If I didn't progress soon then they would need to intervene. I can't labour forever. The consultant wanted to make us aware that a section may be required, we still had some time but she didn't want to just spring it on us at the last minute.

3am and the consultant called it. Nothing was happening, we'd been at this now for nearly 12 hours and nothing had changed. Baby N was back to back which isn't ideal for labour and I'd already had the epidural so let's get her out.

I didn't really know what to expect from a section, but it was so calm. I guess although it was still an emergency section, as in, it wasn't planned, because we had an idea it was coming for the past few hours this alleviated some panic. It certainly wasn't a red button emergency.

My top half (chest and shoulders) were shaking uncontrollably in theatre as if I was cold and shivering but I couldn't stop. The anaesthetist explained how sometimes the epidural can do that to you. I also started to get a really strange sensation in my shoulder and neck, a bit like cramp but it was so strong it made me feel sick. All normal apparently, nothing to worry about.

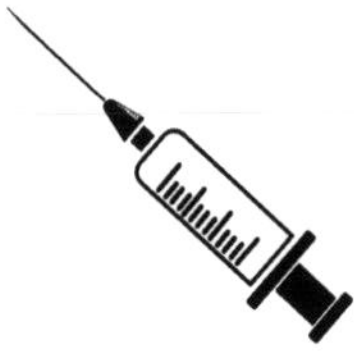

Welcome to the world

Baby N was born, a fabulous pink colour; she needed a rub down to encourage her to cry which is really common with a section delivery. Steve cut the cord and she was placed on my chest so Steve and I could enjoy a snuggle whilst the team put me back together again, ironic considering I definitely resembled humpty dumpty by this point.

Shortly after delivery, Steve and Baby N were taken to the recovery room to wait for me. I was advised that I had lost a concerning amount of blood. The expected amount is approx. 500ml whereas I had lost 1.5L. The team had managed to control the bleeding without me having to have a transfusion but I would now need monitoring more closely.

I was soon reunited with Steve and Baby N, in recovery. We were able to spend a few hours together which was nice, and I was still numb from the epidural so I was thankful I could enjoy our time together pain-free.

Steve had to leave at lunchtime, when I was transferred from recovery onto a ward – obviously I had to stay in hospital for monitoring following my section and due to current Covid restrictions, the ward had put a stop to ALL visitors, meaning Steve now wouldn't see us until we were discharged.

We were gutted, such a magical moment, cut short and taken from us due to the pandemic.

Code Red

I was only on the ward for about half an hour when the emergency button was pressed and my cubicle rapidly turned into a scene you'd expect from a TV show.

I was transferred to a private room and advised I had SEPSIS, and that Baby N & I needed urgent treatment. Due to my high temperature I also had to be treated as suspected Covid, hence the isolation room. Anyone that came into my room had to wear full hazmat suits and masks. I was petrified.

Not only was I frightened for myself but for my new baby, who, because of me, now had to be prodded and poked and required needles and cannulas. It made me feel sick.

One of the worst things about it all was that we were alone. Poor Steve was having to miss all of her first moments, and his worry intensified as he couldn't be with us.

We'd spent years trying to become parents and now he's having to miss her first days, not to mention we needed him now more than ever.

The midwives were amazing, but I was very aware that I wasn't their only patient. I just couldn't rely on them the same way I would with Steve, I missed him terribly and it broke my heart that he was having to miss his new baby.

I have since found out (from the midwives on the ward) that the uncontrollable shaking during my section and the strange sensation in my shoulder, were NOT normal nor are they caused by the epidural. This was the explanation we were given to avoid panic until the team could be sure.

The bleed was true but only added to the concern.

The symptoms I experienced are actually the two most common signs of SEPSIS, so from that moment I was on high alert and thank goodness the team were so quick to spot this.

The Theatre team absolutely saved my life that day.

Our Covid results soon returned negative and Baby N and I were transferred back onto the ward. I was nervous to be around other people with my new baby but it was actually quite nice to talk to others who were in a similar situation to me – we were all alone and missing our partners and naturally turned to each other.

Baby N and I stayed in hospital for 6 days. I will never feel comfortable with this, and I will always blame Covid for stealing this time from both me and Steve.

One last, anger-heavy cocktail complete with a double shot of guilt. A bitterness I couldn't wait to finish.

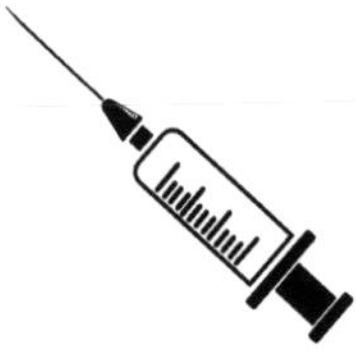

Forever Grateful

I will never again take Steve for granted, well, I probably will, let's be honest, but I'll really try not to.

Not only was he super loving and complimentary during labour, a time when I probably didn't deserve many compliments, but he absolutely gave me everything I needed. Emotionally and physically he couldn't have been more supportive.

He made me feel like superwoman and when I thought I couldn't do it and panicked, he gave me the strength to get me through the panic and forget I was ever frightened.

When he left the hospital he was my absolute rock. I was under no illusions that as much as I had missed him, it must have been so much more heart-breaking for Steve. At least I was with Baby N, that poor man had just met his daughter for the first time and then had to leave her indefinitely.

He didn't spend those days complaining or moaning, he spent them checking I was OK, looking after our house, sending supportive messages, ensuring I was feeling safe and well, caring for us both even when he couldn't be with us.

I couldn't ask for a better husband or best friend and I am so grateful for him.

But don't tell him!!!

Mummy and Daddy

You may have noticed that my last few chapters haven't been date stamped as the previous ones have – this is a small insight into life as a new mummy, you really don't know what day it is.

Every day is filled with love and joy and it is absolutely magical and worth every emotion and all of the physical and emotional pain I had to endure.

The first weeks have been hard, it's scary to be responsible for a life, a new life that you love unconditionally from the moment they are created. My advice is "reach out", take as much help as you can.

My mum has been our saviour and I'd have been lost without her. Moving in with us for the first weeks – due to Covid we couldn't have visitors, so my mum put her life on hold to move in with us and support us.

Don't second guess yourself or put too much pressure on yourself.

You can do it.

We did it.

And god is it worth it when you do!

NEL NICHOLSON
13.05.2020
8LB 11OZ
4:14AM

We promise to spend our lives ensuring
you know just how loved you are.

In an attempt to raise awareness and avoid offence by simply not knowing, I wanted to enlighten you all to some of our insider information within the TTC (trying to conceive) community.

I really tried to refrain from using any of the following within my book as I didn't want to disconnect with anyone outside of the TTC community.

This process is extremely confusing and overwhelming so for those new to the TTC community, use this if required.

I hope the following allows you to better support those you may know that have been affected by fertility/infertility and open the line of communication which can encourage the end of the stigma often associated with infertility.

Rainbow Baby

A rainbow baby is a term used when referring to a child born to a family who have previously lost a child due to miscarriage, stillbirth or death during infancy.

The term "rainbow" is used in reference to how a rainbow appears in the sky following a storm.

These pregnancies can often be misunderstood and to the family can act as triggers and reminders of their previous loss.

Rainbow babies are often confused with IVF babies; these are NOT the same although sometimes a baby can be both rainbow and IVF.

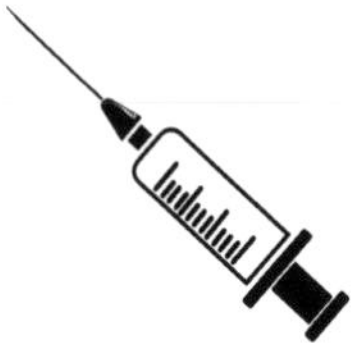

Pineapple

Pineapples have unofficially become the symbol of fertility treatment, particularly IVF.

There are many explanations as to why:

- Unlike most fruits, pineapples are not grown from seeds.

  The pollen of a pineapple plant cannot fertilize members of the same variety and the plant will produce a seedless fruit that develops without fertilization.

  This makes the pineapple the only fruit that requires intervention and assisted fertilisation to reproduce.

- The shape of a pineapple acts as a reminder to people (usually women) undergoing fertility treatment to "stand tall and wear your crown".

- There is also a theory that pineapple (particularly the core) contains bromelain, an enzyme that helps us break down/digest food. If taken on an empty stomach, bromelain can act as an anti-inflammatory or blood thinner; some believe this can help an embryo implant in the uterus.

- Those experiencing fertility struggles and/or undergoing fertility treatment often portray a tough exterior and inherit "pointy", complex defences but remain sweet inside.

- My favourite, and the most humorous of the explanations, is simply that we all deserve a pina colada.

Wearing or displaying a pineapple doesn't have to mean you have or are undergoing IVF. It can act as a welcome sign of support.

People use the pineapple in different ways – sometimes it may be used as a subtle representation of an enormous life event for the person wearing/displaying it. It could also be used as a very obvious, in your face, hard to avoid shout of support to raise awareness.

IVF Treatment Definitions

Artificial Insemination
Artificially inserting sperm into the uterus in order to get pregnant without having sex.

Ampoule
The packaging used to contain the vials of fertility drugs.

Assisted Reproductive Technology
The umbrella term used to collectively describe fertility treatments where both the sperm and egg is handled.

Assisted Hatching
More common following numerous failed attempts of IVF.

A small hole is created to allow the fertilised embryo to "hatch" from the zona pellucida (layer of cells) on the 4th day of development. Hatching from these cells is required to attach to the uterus.

Azoospermia
No sperm present in the semen.

Basal Body Temperature
Your body's natural temperature during rest.

Biochemical Pregnancy
(see also Chemical Pregnancy)
Early miscarriage. Usually within the first few weeks following embryo transfer.

Blastocyst
The term used to describe an embryo on day 5 post-fertilisation. The inner cells eventually develop into the foetus and the outer cells will then form the placenta.

Buserelin
Synthetic hormone drug used to stop your ovaries from working during the start of IVF; another drug is later used to restart your ovaries.

Chemical Pregnancy
Early miscarriage. Usually within the first few weeks following embryo transfer.

Clomid
Fertility drug used to stimulate your ovaries.

Controlled Ovarian Stimulation
Stimulation of the ovaries using fertility drugs such as Clomid.

Cryopreservation
Freezing cells or tissue – the medical term for freezing your eggs/sperm/embryos.

Donor Insemination
Using sperm from a donor for your fertility treatment.

Down Regulation
The term used to describe the period when you are taking drugs to stop your ovaries from working during the start of IVF.

Embryo
The correct name for a baby at 2-8 weeks of development.

Embryo Transfer
The final stage of IVF when your embryo is inserted into your uterus.

Frozen Embryo Transfer
The same process as embryo transfer but with an embryo that has been frozen and thawed.

Follicles
The small liquid-filled sacs in your ovaries that host an immature egg prior to growth and ovulation.

Follicle-Stimulating Hormone
In women this hormone regulates your menstrual cycle.

In men this hormone manages sperm production.

Implantation
The very early stage of pregnancy where the blastocyst attaches to your uterus.

In Vitro
A Latin term referring to a medical procedure that happens outside the body.

Menopur
A fertility drug used to stimulate your ovaries. This drug contains HCG.

Natural Cycle IVF
The IVF procedure without the use of fertility drugs to manipulate the cycle, no down regulation; this version of IVF is completely reliant on your natural cycle.

Ovarian Hyperstimulation Syndrome
A potential complication of the fertility drugs.

Ovum
Another name for an egg.

Sperm Washing
Separating sperm from semen.

Zygote
The result of combining the egg and sperm for fertilising. The cell produced is called a Zygote and this eventually becomes the embryo.

Abbreviations

2WW: Two week wait

AF: Aunt Flo, period/menstrual cycle

ART: Assisted reproductive technology
(for example: IVF)

BBT: Basal body temperature

BCP: Birth control pills

Beta: HCG test

BFN: Big fat negative

BFP: Big fat positive

CB: Cycle buddy

CD: Cycle day

DE: Donor eggs

DH: Dear husband

DI: Donor husband

DOR: Diminished ovarian reserve

DPO: Days post-ovulation

DPR: Days post-retrieval

DPT: Days post-transfer

DW: Dear wife

Dx: Diagnosis

ENDO: Endometriosis

EPT: Early pregnancy test

ER: Egg retrieval

ET: Embryo transfer

FET: Frozen embryo transfer

FF: Fertility friend

FHR: Foetal heart rate

FSH: Follicle-stimulating hormone

FTTA: Fertility thoughts to all

HCG:
Human chronic gonadotropin
(the hormone detected by a pregnancy test)

HPT: Home pregnancy test

HSG: Hysterosalpingogram

HX: History

ICSI: Intracytoplasmic sperm injection

IF: Infertility

IR: Insulin resistant

IVF: In-vitro fertilisation

IUI: Intrauterine insemination

LAP: Laparoscopy

LH: Luteinizing hormone

LMP: Last menstrual period (last start date)

LSP: Low sperm count

MAI: Miscarriage after infertility

MC: Miscarriage

MF: Male factor

O, OV: Ovulation

OB, OB/GYN: Obstetrician/Gynaecologist

OC: Oral contraception

OPK/OPT: Ovulation predictor kit/ Ovulation predictor test

OTC: Over the counter

PCOS: Polycystic Ovarian Syndrome

PG: Pregnant

PGD/PGS: Pre-implantation genetic diagnosis/ Pre-implantation genetic screening

PI: Primary infertility

PIO: Progesterone in oil injection

PID: Pelvic Inflammatory Disease

POAS: Pee on a stick

POF: Premature ovarian failure

PUPO: Pregnant until proven otherwise

RE: Reproductive endocrinologist

RPL: Recurrent pregnancy loss

SA: Semen analysis

SART: Society for Assisted Reproductive
Technology

SI: Secondary infertility

TL/TR: Tubal ligation/Tubal reversal

TTC: Trying to conceive

TTCAR: Trying to conceive after reversal

TWW: Two week wait

TX: Treatment

US: Ultrasound

V/VR: Vasectomy/Vasectomy reversal